"In *The Riches of Your Grace*, Julie Lane-Gay models for us how Archbishop Thomas Cranmer, along with the Anglican divines, intended Anglicans across the centuries to use the Book of Common Prayer. She will enrich the spiritual lives of many by sharing this testimony of the immense benefit she has derived from such joyful engagement with the prayer book. This work will encourage those who are struggling spiritually, emotionally, and relationally in their walk with Jesus; it will help frazzled believers find their spiritual footing in our frenetic world. I highly recommend this book to the church and to those who are seeking to find their way back to God."
Felix Orji, bishop of the Anglican Diocese of All Nations, Anglican Church in North America

"'Something deep and sturdy' is how Julie Lane-Gay characterized the power resident in the Anglican Book of Common Prayer when she was first invited to make it a part of her daily life. As a mother of children and editor at Regent College, her times of devotional reading and prayer were limited. But in this glowing new book she details how the seminal ancient prayers and responses of the prayer book began to sink into her spirit, becoming as warm and powerful as glowing coals as they fed her burgeoning spiritual life."
Luci Shaw, author of *Reversing Entropy* and *The O in Hope*

"Something utterly unexpected is happening to many North American Christians. They are discovering that a book nearly five hundred years old is having a deep, rich, and strengthening impact on them and their relationship with almighty God. Julie Lane-Gay's book is a gem. In it she describes her journey with the Book of Common Prayer and how God used it to teach her deeper truths about herself and ourselves. This book will become a treasure to countless people who are finding their way along the Anglican path in God's kingdom. It should be given to all new members in our churches."
John W Yates II, rector of The Falls Church Anglican, retired

"Beautifully written and disarmingly honest, Julie Lane-Gay's book is a gift. You will identify with her longing for a rhythm in her worship and personal prayer life. You'll want to join her in her discovery of how the Book of Common Prayer gives us a framework for words we struggle to pray. This is not a guide on how to pray better but a vista of a lay person's real life, a life like yours and mine. Grab copies for yourself and for all your people!"
Susan Alexander Yates, speaker and author of *Risky Faith*

"Julie Lane-Gay has given us a one-of-a-kind introduction to the Book of Common Prayer. She takes us through the book as it has intersected with her life, providing some of the book's historical context along the way. Each chapter takes us to a different section of the book, like a tour guide who describes destinations and is personally familiar with all the stops. Julie knows the prayer book intimately and shares candid and often poignant moments when it has deepened her life with God and others. I have used the prayer book for decades, but she reacquainted me with aspects of it that I had not often visited and in ways that show me how it connects with our daily lives."
Dennis Okholm, professor emeritus at Azusa Pacific University and author of *Monk Habits for Everyday People*

"Julie Lane Gay has provided us an exquisite guide to the Book of Common Prayer—demonstrating its formative power for both the shared worship of the church and in our personal prayers. She shows how it can foster within us and among us the capacity to live in the grace of God in a post-Christian and secular age, and further, how this ancient Anglican resource is a potential gift to Christians of all theological and spiritual traditions."
Gordon Smith, president of Ambrose University in Calgary, Alberta, and author of *Courage and Calling*

"There are, happily, now a number of how-to guides for using the Book of Common Prayer from the Anglican tradition of Christianity. But this book is something different: more of a warm invitation than a simple instruction manual. It is a disarming personal testimony of a spiritual life lived with the prayer book and a hospitable summons for others to experience the rich gifts of that life."

Wesley Hill, priest in the Episcopal Church and associate professor of New Testament at Western Theological Seminary in Holland, Michigan

"Julie Lane-Gay is guide and fellow explorer in this rich contemplation of the Book of Common Prayer. Her personal journey through an ancient text of Anglicanism is honest and poetic. As she reads the Book of Common Prayer at church and at home, the book reads her, and we all benefit. The Book of Common Prayer can at first seem formal and a bit complicated for some of us, but in Lane-Gay's skilled and sensitive hands, we experience how it opens the mysteries of God's grace, love, and direction in our daily lives. I put down this book and felt encouraged to pick up that 'small red book' once again."

Karen Stiller, author of *Holiness Here: Searching for God in the Ordinary Events of Everyday Life* and *The Minister's Wife: A Memoir of Faith, Doubt, Friendship, Loneliness, Forgiveness, and More*

"For almost five hundred years, the Book of Common Prayer has been one of the Anglican Church's great gifts to God's church around the world, drawing its readers into the Jesus-centered, true worship of God. *The Riches of Your Grace* is a wonderful, wise, warm, informative, and down-to-earth invitation into the treasures of the Anglican prayer book. Julie's Lane-Gay's theological insight and deep appreciation for the profound way that the Book of Common Prayer helps people draw near to God in real life today shines through this captivating book. I give it the highest of recommendations."

Dan Gifford, diocesan bishop of the Anglican Network in Canada

"On my shelf are many guides, handbooks, and histories of the Book of Common Prayer, but Julie Lane-Gay has offered something refreshingly different from these. She knows this background and draws on it skillfully, but more than this, she shows us from her own experience what it means, from the inside, for one's real life to be shaped by the rhythms of the prayer book. There is nothing stuffy here. Julie's compelling personal narrative is all about how these ancient words seep into you, little by little, and change you at the very depths of your being. *The Riches of Your Grace* is a winsome companion to prayer book worship in everyday life."

Bruce Hindmarsh, James M. Houston Professor of Spiritual Theology at Regent College in Vancouver, British Columbia, and author of *The Spirit of Early Evangelicalism*

"*The Riches of Your Grace* offers a deeply personal encounter with the liturgical and sacramental treasures of the Book of Common Prayer. Reclaiming the lost art of devotional writing, Julie Lane-Gay shows how the structure and discipline of Anglican common prayer do not leave us with a rote piety; the prayers nurture deep intimacy both with the living Lord and in our life together as his body. Church libraries will bless their parishes with a copy on their shelves."

Kathryn Greene-McCreight, priest affiliate at Christ Church New Haven and author of *Darkness Is My Only Companion*

"Julie Lane-Gay has written a book that weaves an accessible explanation of the practices of the Book of Common Prayer into a narrative of her own life, described with such simple candor that we can easily feel she is talking about us or those we dearly love. She has done this with vivid images—sights, sounds, smells—using just the right amount of words, so that this book is not only eminently readable but artistically beautiful. She has prepared and presented this feast well! The result is a testimony of the transformative power of the Book of Common Prayer that invites us to partake in the feast ourselves."

Steven Breedlove, bishop of the Anglican Diocese of Christ Our Hope in the eastern United States

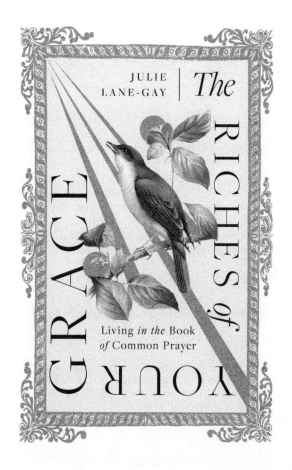

JULIE
LANE-GAY | *The*

RICHES *of*

GRACE

YOUR

Living *in the* Book
of Common Prayer

An imprint of InterVarsity Press
Downers Grove, Illinois

InterVarsity Press
P.O. Box 1400 | Downers Grove, IL 60515-1426
ivpress.com | email@ivpress.com

InterVarsity Press® is the publishing division of InterVarsity Christian Fellowship/USA®. For more information, visit www.intervarsity.org.

All Scripture quotations, unless otherwise indicated, are taken from The Holy Bible, New International Version®, NIV®. Copyright © 1973, 1978, 1984, 2011 by Biblica, Inc.™ Used by permission of Zondervan. All rights reserved worldwide. www.zondervan.com. The "NIV" and "New International Version" are trademarks registered in the United States Patent and Trademark Office by Biblica, Inc.™

Scripture quotations for all psalms are taken from The Book of Common Prayer with the New Coverdale Psalter. Copyright © 2019 by the Anglican Church in North America. The New Coverdale Psalter Copyright © 2019 by the Anglican Church in North America.

While any stories in this book are true, names and identifying information have been changed to protect the privacy of individuals.

The publisher cannot verify the accuracy or functionality of website URLs used in this book beyond the date of publication.

Cover design: David Fassett
Interior design: Daniel van Loon
Cover images: © Andrew_Howe / E+ via Getty Images, Abadal I Fontcuberta, Josep, Circa Artist, Pau Abadal I Fontcuberta, Ignasi Abadal I Girifau, Pere Abadal I Morató, and Andreu Abadal I Serra. Abadal Album of Samples. Catalonia Manresa Spain Moià, 1800. [place of publication not identified: Abadal Family] Photograph. https://www.loc.gov/item/2021670720/.

ISBN 978-1-5140-0816-4 (print) | ISBN 978-1-5140-0817-1 (digital)

Printed in the United States of America ∞

Library of Congress Cataloging-in-Publication Data
Names: Lane-Gay, Julie, 1959- author.
Title: The riches of your grace : living in the Book of common prayer / Julie Lane-Gay.
Description: Downers Grove, IL : IVP, [2024]	Includes bibliographical references.
Identifiers: LCCN 2023054874 (print)	LCCN 2023054875 (ebook)	ISBN 9781514008164 (print)	ISBN 9781514008171 (digital)
Subjects: LCSH: Church of England. Book of common prayer.	BISAC: RELIGION / Christian Living / Personal Memoirs	BIOGRAPHY & AUTOBIOGRAPHY / Personal Memoirs
Classification: LCC BX5145 .L35 2024 (print)	LCC BX5145 (ebook)
LC record available at https://lccn.loc.gov/2023054874
LC ebook record available at https://lccn.loc.gov/2023054875

31 30 29 28 27 26 25 24 | 12 11 10 9 8 7 6 5 4 3 2 1

FOR MAXINE AND THENA

a small token of enormous thanks

.

AND FOR CRAIG

who shares the riches of the prayer book,

and His grace, so wisely

CONTENTS

INTRODUCTION

*N*early fifteen years ago, I was at a weekend retreat off the coast of Washington—there were wood cabins, homey food, occasional views of the snowcapped Olympic mountains. Good friends were the speakers, and I went largely to hear and support them. On the wet Saturday morning, colorful raincoats draped and dripping over unused chairs, we were divided into groups of eight and asked that we go around the circle sharing our names, telling where we were from, and answering the question, "What has shaped you as a Christian?"

My stomach tightened hearing the last question, and more so as my turn got closer. Was I pathetic not to know? The complete absence of faith in my childhood? The books of C. S. Lewis? Our group's leader clearly wanted something more specific than "the Holy Spirit" or "Scripture." As the woman two to my left was telling us about her time working in Uganda, I suddenly realized my answer. The Book of Common Prayer. It was a surprise—and made total sense.

Week after week, in the pews at church, praying at home with the small red book, texting a collect to my sister late at night, the prayer book's words had steadied and shaped me. When my kids were small and I was too weary to form a coherent thought, when marriage was so hard I wanted to give up, when my sin felt so acute I was too ashamed to pray, when I knew I was supposed to praise God but felt little enthusiasm, the prayer book was my life preserver. Its words of grace and confession, its prayers in their set patterns, have been the primary means of God's love and grace to me.

When it was my turn and I answered, "the Book of Common Prayer," there were raised eyebrows and perplexed stares. Was it strange that a 450-year-old British book could have that capacity? Did my circle-mates find it odd that I had been shaped by saying the same antiquated words every Sunday? I was dressed in my green fleece and faded jeans, but perhaps they thought the prayer book was only for people who wore tweed jackets and read dead English poets.

I knew my answer was true—and the more I have reflected on it since that rainy morning, the more I know I was given a gift. The language *is* old, and the prayers are set, but the prayer book has been constant in showing me God's tender understanding of my heart and in conveying His loving character and steady presence— for being what the prayer book calls a "means of grace and hope of glory."

Theologian Lesslie Newbigin writes, "The business of the church is to tell and embody a story."[1] I would add the church's business is also to watch for that story, to watch for God at work in the world, to be like my sky-watching husband who stays up into the early hours of the morning looking for a galaxy. The prayer book has been my window on that story, showing me God in our midst and leading me to become more skilled at doing so. The prayer book hasn't become a substitute for the Bible but a means to live into it.

⟐

I first picked up a prayer book when my husband, Craig, and I went on a short trip to western Canada. Amid spectacular hikes and salmon dinners, we decided to attend an Anglican church near where we were staying. In my early twenties, I had no idea what the words "Anglican" or "Episcopal" meant, much less that the people in the pews followed a set liturgy, a script between a pastor and the congregation that was laid out in a historic prayer book. The book intimidated me. The old words—*thy* and *beseech* and *manifold*—felt pretentious and old-fashioned. There were so many directions in italics. Which page were we on? Where was the spontaneity? The joy? Why were the leaders in front dressed in long black robes, and why did they repeatedly get down on the ground to kneel? How did anyone know when to stand or kneel? What was an Absolution? The Lectionary? The Creed?

But as we concluded Holy Communion (was it okay that we went forward to receive it?), I was also amazed. Moving through the script—the progression of confession, Scripture, praise—the service had prepared us for this meal; we didn't jump right in. As we knelt to have the body and the blood of Christ placed in our cupped hands, the magnitude of the gift sank deep.

To my surprise, our feelings and responses were not the focus of the service, nor were the pastors. The only personality we attended to was God's. Instead of my trying to create enthusiastic, thankful feelings toward Him, I recognized that God was initiating, waiting for us. We were responding. When we knelt and prayed, "Almighty God, unto whom all hearts be open, all desires known, and from whom no secrets are hid," I felt I was handed the world's best invitation—to sink into God's arms just as I was. Even as the worship felt awkward, it ministered to my longing.

Several years later when we began to attend an Anglican church regularly, the archaic words and prayers started to draw me in rather than distance me. I had a sense I was joining into something deep and sturdy.

My passion in life is plants—be it pines, roses, or daisies. I study them, grow them, find experts on them, love them. And as I have done so (Craig might say, as I have obsessively done so), I have learned their language, the Linnaean system of naming (and often describing) plants in Latin. Pines are all *pinus*, but there are 126 different kinds of *pinus*, 126 different species. *Pinus longaeva* is the Bristlecone—it's the oldest, and the Latin means "ancient." It is far easier to know the personalities of pines, and all plants, when you understand something about their Latin names; when you know to whom they are related. It places them in the world of trees, within all plants. So it has been with the old words of the liturgy. They have become not only a blessing, but a means of context, of learning.

As Craig and I participated in the services week after week, we memorized their words without even trying. The *thys* and *thees* and *beseeches* became part of the prayer book's song; the poetry deepening meanings rather than distancing me. The lyricism began to find its way into different parts of me; as a friend says, "sidling into my right brain as well as my left."

I soon borrowed a prayer book from the back of the church (I have yet to return it) and began pulling it out when I knew I needed to pray. It felt easier than thinking up apt words myself. I said a collect as I headed out the door in the morning, and before I started work. When I went to bed, I plunked my worries into His keeping as I said, "Preserve us, O God, waking, and guard us sleeping, that awake we may watch with Christ, and asleep we may rest in peace." I began praying more frequently because I didn't have to conjure up the words.

Hearing the preambles to the prayers that began with the attributes of who God is, "who is always to have mercy," "who of thy tender love towards mankind, has sent thy savior, Jesus Christ," transformed my experience of knowing His love. I wasn't learning of God's love through the direct statement "God loves you." I was learning of his love through the qualities that emanated from Him.

I assumed that saying the same words over and over, week after week (and eventually day after day), would soon feel contrived; that I wasn't being honest with God. But again, I was surprised. In saying the Lord's Prayer repeatedly, I saw more of its brilliance, not less. In saying the Confession each week, I became more honest, more specific. And unlike scrolling on my phone (which I also do repeatedly), saying the words of the prayer book brought hope and deep goodness into my parched heart. Hearing myself say the prayers, hearing others say them, reiterates that God knows me and loves me deeply. The prayers convey over and over how relational God is. These are words I *want* to hear over and over.

Not long after that weekend retreat, a tall athletic fellow who had been in my group asked me if I had ever considered using the Celtic Book of Daily Prayer. "What made you pick the Anglican prayer book?" he wondered. I admitted while I was aware of the Celtic Book of Daily Prayer (and the Northumbrian community that has shared it with the world), I had never looked for a system of prayer. I fell into the prayer book and stayed. The more it pulled me closer to God, to the love of Christ, I didn't want to let it go. I have occasionally read parts of other "systems," such as Phyllis Tickle's collections of daily prayers, *The Divine Hours* (I love that she organized the prayers by season), Paul Miller's "index cards" method, and *Common Prayer: A Liturgy for Ordinary Radicals* with its great assortment of historic prayers and readings in contemporary language. I've enjoyed and learned from them all. But I have stuck close to the Anglican Book of Common Prayer, not only for its thorough rootedness in Scripture but also for how pointedly it speaks to my personal longings (and insecurities) and for its magnitude. The prayer book anchors every day of the year, every Sunday in worship, every season, every birth and death and in between. Knowing the same prayers are being said each Sunday in Rio, Rotterdam, and Reno, and have been said for hundreds of years before me, holds me in the community of God's people, in God's story.

Thirty years after being intimidated and awkward, being lost amid the words of the Te Deum and the Venite, the prayer book is now in my knapsack, my glovebox, my office drawer, my iPad. When I feel anxious about the demands ahead, I hastily say the Collect for Peace. When I hear my husband, kneeling next to me, saying the General Confession, "We have followed too much the devices and desires of our own hearts," I find it far easier to forgive him for snapping at me in the car; the Confession has shown me that I am often the one who's rude first.

Over time I have become what my kids describe as "big" on the prayer book. Several years ago I took a class on the Psalms and the professor was speaking about the need for our worship to "catechize us," to teach us about God, about His work in the world. I saw my opportunity and called out, "We need the Book of Common Prayer!" A good friend laughed at my predictability and said, "Julie is like the kids at the children's time in church. When the minister asks the kids a question, the answer is always 'Jesus!' Julie's answer is always 'the prayer book!'"

⟞⟜⟠⟜⟞

I'm not a priest, historian, or theologian. I am not inclined to prayer and I am not naturally disciplined. This book is not a guide (a friend teased me that it's more like an "enlarged travel brochure"). It's a vista of a layperson living in the prayer book, one who is still learning. I want to help you be more comfortable with it, blessed by what you're participating in. I've included history and instructions here and there, but mostly I have tried to show how the age-old prayers and liturgies have drawn me, and others, closer to God, how we have become more attentive to Him, and how He has drawn closer to us.

The prayer book still intimidates me. Some parts still mystify me. Finding my way through the vast number of versions of the Anglican and Episcopal Books of Common Prayer, printed from 1542 to 2019, occasionally overwhelms me. Editions have been updated for language, pertinence, and theology. There are versions that use words and phrases appropriate to 1662, such as "heartily sorry for these our misdoings, The remembrance of them is grievous unto us; the burthen of them is intolerable," and others that use the language of 2019, rendering the same phrase as "deeply sorry for these our transgressions; the burden of them is more than we can bear."

To further complicate this plethora, there are different editions of the prayer book in England, Canada, Singapore, New Zealand, Kenya, the United States, and elsewhere.

One silver lining amid these versions of time and location is the similarity of what's in them; the order of the table of contents is relatively similar between versions. Almost all prayer books begin with the daily prayers (what most of us would say at home) titled as the Daily Office. These are the services of Morning, Midday, and Evening Prayer. Some versions include Compline (the service just before bed) and the Litany (a service of intercessory prayer). The second section of almost all prayer books covers the two services of the Sacraments: Baptism and Holy Communion. These are always communal, to be done in a church community with a priest leading us through them. The next section of the prayer book is the "pastoral rites"—the gigantic moments—services for marriage, children, and dying. The fourth section is usually the Psalter, offering all 150 psalms (in order) but separating them into a morning and evening reading for each day of the month; it's the longest section in the prayer book. The Psalter is followed by the services related to church life, such as the ordination of deacons, priests, bishops, and archbishops and the sanctifying of a church building or a graveyard.

I was recently at the service where one of our parish priests was being ordained to become the bishop of Canada. The service was held in a large church filled with countless clergy in long white gowns, greeting each other with hugs and laughter (I silently wondered if Dumbledore was there too). A tall, gold shepherd's crook was carried up to the altar and vast candles flickered luminously. We were all there to witness Dan make momentous vows. In a loud but humble voice, he promised to "renounce all ungodliness and worldly lusts, and live a godly, righteous and sober life in this present world," to show himself "in all things an example of good works for others, that the adversary may be ashamed, having nothing to say against you." It made marriage vows look easy.

The final sections of the prayer book guide us through the Liturgical Year with a collect for each week of the year and the designated Bible readings for each day throughout the year (the Lectionary).

To squeeze all this in, most prayer books are more than seven hundred pages long.

Living in Canada for most of my adult life (that first visit turned into a long stay), the 1962 Canadian Book of Common Prayer has been the one on my desk and in my car, but there are equally good ones across the world.[2] For weekly worship, my own church weaves together the 1962 edition, the 2019 Anglican Church in North America (ACNA) edition, and occasionally the 1662 edition. Again, it's confusing. In this book I have generally quoted either the 2019 ACNA edition or the Canadian 1962 edition. My hope is that the chapters will focus on the similarities of these versions, minimize the confusion, and most importantly, give you confidence that you can find your way.

As I tell those navigating their way into the prayer book, there are no liturgical speed traps. No one is waiting to catch you. No one will be upset if you read the wrong prayer at the wrong time, stand at the wrong time—or if you forget to use the prayer book at all.

May this book be a friendly welcome mat, an encouragement to venture into the prayer book's pages, into its rhythms and prayers, into God's abundant wisdom, love, and grace, into His amazing and trustworthy Story.

1

MORNING *and* EVENING PRAYER

I'm late yet again.

I pull in behind the police station (where parking is free on Sundays) and race over to our tall, sandstone church. I wish I'd gotten here earlier to hear the musical prelude. The music quiets me, gives my soul a little breathing room. It's worth getting out of the house five minutes earlier but I'm lousy at doing that.

The foyer runs along the back of the sanctuary and Tricia, warm and good-humored, opens the side door and hands me my bulletin. I must look sheepish because she shrugs and smiles in a way that says, "Don't sweat it. You aren't the only one who is late. You got here." Her kindness softens me for worship.

The sanctuary is almost full. Soccer moms, university professors, bartenders, and computer programmers fill the pews. There are shorts and ripped T-shirts and dark suits with neckties. Depending on the season, rain boots, Adidas, and flip-flops abound. Like me, these people can be self-absorbed and high maintenance, but when cancer erupts, kids are arrested, jobs are lost, or spouses cheat, they are right there with you.

There are no wood-hewn beams or stone pillars; no stunning stained-glass windows. It's not the Canterbury Cathedral. The organ is adequate; the piano might be better. The choir is wonderful but there are not a hundred cherubic children in white robes with perfect pitch. With its sturdy tan pews and red carpeting, the sanctuary is comfortable at best. I've come to value its ordinariness; it doesn't inspire awe, but when you track in a bit of mud or a baby cries during the sermon, no one feels like they're ruining anything. It's never a performance.

As I move across a middle row to sit closer to the center, I squeeze the shoulders of our friends Michelle and Ben in the pew in front of me and get acknowledging smiles. It comforts me to find them week after week, year after year. I hope I'm that presence for others.

My jacket barely off, the congregation settles back onto the pews as the organ's last notes of the opening hymn fade. This morning's service is Morning Prayer, and while the prayer book compilers intended the service to be said daily (and many do say it daily), our church is unusual in that we alternate on Sundays, celebrating Holy Communion on the second and fourth Sundays of the month and Morning Prayer on the first and third. It's an oddity I've come to appreciate.

Some people say the services of Morning and Evening Prayer (together called the Daily Office) each day at home. In the early days of the Covid-19 pandemic, a number of people at our church gathered online twice a day to say these services together, and they have carried on ever since. They take turns leading and reading the Scriptures. I continue to hear it described as a "lifeline" and a "crucial framework for my day."

The Daily Office has a deep history. Long before Christ, the Jewish people voiced their prayers of praise and sacrifice in the temple at 9:00 a.m. and 3:00 p.m.; they knew that their rituals were what taught and formed them.

Some days at home, I say Morning Prayer by myself. Sitting at the kitchen table or my desk, I read it like a script, saying all the parts and prayers aloud. It was awkward till I got used to it, until hearing the words mattered more than the clumsiness. Some days I don't get to all the Scriptures; too often I just read the Psalms.

The Daily Office offers a way to shape our workdays and remind us who we are—created, known, and loved by God, people whose work is prayer. It gives us a way to move closer to Scripture's encouragement to "pray without ceasing."

⁂

Our rector (or head pastor) begins this morning's liturgy with the Opening Sentence, a call to worship that sets the tone for all that we are about to do. He reads, "I was glad when they said unto me, 'We will go into the house of the LORD'" (Psalm 122:1). It offers a transition from the parking lot to worship, but it also contains an important acknowledgment. Pastor Tim Challies writes,

> The Call to Worship is a means of acknowledging that God's people come to church each week weary, dry, and discouraged. They have laboured through another week and need to be reminded of the rest Christ offers their weary souls. They have endured another week of trials, temptations, or persecutions and come thirsty, eager to drink the water of life and to be refreshed by it. They have walked another seven days of their journey as broken, sinful people and need to be reminded of who Christ is and who they are in him. Church is urgent business! Instead of being asked how they are, Christians need to be reminded who they are. Instead of being asked where everyone else is, Christians need to be reminded where Christ is.[1]

Chosen according to the church calendar (or Liturgical Year), the Opening Sentences vary by the seasons of Advent, Christmas,

Epiphany, Lent, Easter, and Pentecost. This calendar marks our days and months within the eternal rather than the pragmatic. As poet Malcolm Guite says, the church calendar offers a way of "sacralizing time,"[2] of shifting us to see Christ's birth, Baptism, ministry, death, burial, and resurrection both in the past and in our midst.

In the much older versions of the prayer book, the Opening Sentences tended to focus on penitence. Services began with verses such as "I will set out and go back to my father and say to him: Father, I have sinned against heaven and against you. I am no longer worthy to be called your son" (Luke 15:18-19). The intent with this emphasis was to start with the bad news of our sin and set us on the path to repentance and to grace, to remind us that from the outset, absolution and grace are always waiting.

After the Opening Sentences, our rector declares the Call to Confession (some prayer books call this the Exhortation). Before we can praise God, hear His Word, or even thank Him, we need God's grace, we need the reminder that everything in our relationship with Him comes by His grace. The rector reads:

> Dearly beloved, the Scriptures teach us to acknowledge our many sins and offenses, not concealing them from our heavenly Father, but confessing them with humble and obedient hearts that we may obtain forgiveness by his infinite goodness and mercy. We ought at all times humbly to acknowledge our sins before Almighty God, but especially when we come together in his presence to give thanks for the great benefits we have received at his hands, to declare his most worthy praise, to hear his holy Word, and to ask, for ourselves and on behalf of others, those things which are necessary for our life and our salvation. Therefore, draw near with me to the throne of heavenly grace.[3]

"Draw near with me" is always a bonus. I'm not the only one who came through the sanctuary's doors this morning immersed in myself.

Sometimes I make a small, silent addition to the ending of the Exhortation—"Lord, show me mine." I try to make myself ask, "Lord, where have I sinned? What did I do, and what did I not do? Show me where I need to repent." God's answers come more frequently than I would expect and often surprise me—a conversation when I wasn't really listening, a comment in which I tweaked the truth about myself to impress someone. I have come to find it a great sign of God's love that He shows me my sin when I ask.

While it once was daunting, naming my sins has become a means of grace, a means to know its riches. Sin explains the mess of the world, thousands of years ago and this morning. We aren't expected to heal ourselves, only to be humble and ask for God's help. Phrases such as "our many sins and offenses" (in older prayer books it's our "manifold sins and wickedness") and "with a humble and obedient heart" now land on me with relief. "Sins" and "wickedness" are countercultural words, but they bring life-giving freedom. They remind me that we live in a thoroughly fallen world, and they pull me again to seek God's forgiveness.

Some years ago there was a media outcry in the United Kingdom when, in planning his wedding with Camilla Parker Bowles, Prince Charles insisted on keeping this Exhortation in their ceremony, including the words "manifold sins and wickedness." People were horrified. Surely in light of his earlier affair with Camilla, the prince ought to eliminate the language once and for all, naming the affair as something other than "sin."

Charles apparently said that to the contrary, this was the right language for their actions, and the best way to begin his new marriage.[4]

❧❧❧

The first time I participated in the service of Morning Prayer, I was visiting to hear a famous preacher. Still happy with the contemporary worship in the church we attended, the set pattern of worship again felt like work. The service guide filled nine pages with small print. Listening to the pastor's calls and saying the responses, we again seemed to skip some parts and say others. There were hymns and songs at seemingly random times. I worried Morning Prayer would take several hours.

But I also noticed that the scripted dialogue between the pastor and the congregation—the liturgy—was again restful. The service was not about expressing what I was feeling toward God, nor was it about the pastor's entertaining style. The service's words and music and dialogue expressed Christ to me, pouring His love and redemption into each of us. Saying the age-old words that carried such scriptural depth, I felt a relief at not having to conjure up piety or weightiness on my own. There was an intentionality I felt more than understood.

I began to wonder if the contemporary service Craig and I attended was missing something. As Scripture says to us over and over, "Remember!" I was seeing in these scripted prayers and patterns of worship what I frequently skipped over: what God had done in the past and the glorious future ahead.

I was hearing the good news of the gospel not only in the sermon and prayers but in the pattern of the prayers, their content and their sequence. I began to see that the parts of this service were created as a whole. They were steps placed in an order that enabled me to practice behaving like a person who was following Christ, and hopefully over time, with the presence of the Holy Spirit, become like that person from the inside out.

Following the steps of the pattern brought a change in my vantage point, as if I had climbed down an embankment and gotten onto a barge on a big flowing river to experience the land from a new perspective. In this liturgy I was participating in a different narrative of the world, a different telling of its story. Again I sensed the change more than I understood it.

All societies have ways that we "narrate" the world to make sense of it and structure how we live in it. As pastor Eugene Peterson wrote, "We keep sane by telling stories. . . . Stories tell us who we are, tell us what we can do."[5] One of the most common stories we tell in Western society might be summarized as "hope in progress," that with every advance in science and technology, our lives can and will keep getting better. Electric cars, stem cell treatments, finely tuned antidepressants, and personal investing will provide the power and capacity to make our lives easier and happier, even healthier. Rich and poor alike can be healed from cancer and Covid-19. With all the recent advances, children can be better cared for and become better adults.

But as much as I like air travel, antibiotics, and instant messaging, these technologies aren't solving the deeper problems of our world or our hearts. We aren't becoming better or happier people, or sadly, better parents.

As Christians, we have been given a different narrative from the one that says science and technology will consistently keep making things better. We don't get to make up our narrative, or even amend it. It comes to us. The Christian story of the world is God creating, our rebelling, God redeeming in Christ and His coming back to restore all things as they were meant to be. It is both hard to see this story and, once you look carefully, hard to miss it. Our world was created with stunning beauty and brilliance—trees, mountains, whales, dragonflies, and newborn babies show this in abundance, and consistently, but we have messed it all up with our selfishness and greed. God has given us His own Son to redeem us, to save us from the ultimate consequences of what we have done, and He's committed to one day restoring us and our world.

The great advances can be helpful tools, but they do not save us or even love us; they rarely meet our longings to be known, loved, and cherished, to know God is personally with us, waiting for us.

Philosopher Jamie Smith says that this naming, these liturgies of a different sort, can "carry within them a kind of ultimate orientation. . . . They bend the needle of our hearts."[6]

Morning Prayer began to bend mine.

❦❦❦

Following the Call to Confession Exhortation, our congregation lowers themselves onto the red cushions beneath us. We kneel, acting out our script with our bodies as well as our words. Jackets rustle, rain boots squeak, and heavy soles scuff the floor. There's a communal thump—a settling that always signals "home" to me. This is what my people sound like. We're readying ourselves to confess together, to do something we agree we need to do, and that we need to do on our knees. We aren't here to be entertained, we are here to participate. Together we say:

Almighty and most merciful Father, we have erred and strayed from your ways like lost sheep. We have followed too much the devices and desires of our own hearts. We have offended against your holy laws. We have left undone those things which we ought to have done, and we have done those things which we ought not to have done; and apart from your grace, there is no health in us. O Lord, have mercy upon us. Spare all those who confess their faults. Restore all those who are penitent, according to your promises declared to all people in Christ Jesus our Lord. And grant, O most merciful Father, for his sake, that we may now live a godly, righteous, and sober life, to the glory of your holy Name. Amen.[7]

If the Call to Confession is strongly worded, the General Confession is more so. There is no "if I have strayed . . . if I have left undone." We don't say, "some days there is not always health in us."

With its steady beat of one-syllable words, the General Confession embodies gravitas. Kneeling, my soul sinks more into what we are doing—confessing how we have hurt God, each other, the planet. The staccato words—*erred, strayed, lost, sheep, things*—followed by multi-syllable verbs—followed, offended—create a rhythm that stays in our minds. The clauses of the General Confession have been quoted in novels, films, Supreme Court decisions, and tweets because these clauses resonate so pointedly, and as we pray them together, the words build the magnitude of what we are doing: confessing our sins to God Almighty. Like poetry, the paradox of the simplicity of the words and the weightiness of the content keeps the deep truths going not just to our intellects but straight to our hearts.

My mind zips around as I say the Confession. Even as I confess, my sin abounds. Some mornings I wonder, "Did I already do something this morning that I have to ask forgiveness for? Wouldn't confession be better left to Evening Prayer, after I have sinned all day?"

But then I remember. I had an array of very unkind thoughts about a friend who had texted me all night. I was critical of other drivers on my way to church (it was their fault I was late)—all before I got here this morning. Sin starts early.

As we ask God to restore those who are penitent, I try to name not just my sins that have affected the people around me, but my part in the sins that have wounded the world. As priest Noah Van Neil observes, "Individual sin leads to corporate sin. And if we do not confront the sin at the center of our hearts, we will not make much progress on the sins at the center of our society."[8]

Some versions of the General Confession conclude with the wonderful line, "forgive us, that we might delight in your will and walk in your ways." God doesn't give us His grace so that we will buck up and serve, but to delight in His will, in His abundant forgiveness—to enjoy His goodness.

The General Confession is always followed by the Absolution, the proclamation of our complete forgiveness. I always hope the rector will pause after my favorite line, "He pardons and absolves all who truly repent and genuinely believe his holy Gospel" so I can take in the immediacy a bit more.[9] We are never left hanging, wondering if we will be forgiven, if He will only forgive our less harmful sins. God is waiting to forgive. The inseparability of the Confession and Absolution is one of the finest ways the prayer book obliterates any sense that we go to church to get beaten into shame. Anglican priest Tish Harrison Warren writes:

> Confession and absolution must find its way into the small moments of sinfulness in my day. When it does, the gospel—grace itself—seeps into my day, and these moments are transformed. They're no longer meaningless interruptions, sheer failure and lostness and brokenness. Instead, there are moments of redemption and remembering, moments to grow bit by bit in trusting Jesus' work on my behalf.[10]

Since sometimes I say Morning Prayer by myself, I once asked theologian and Anglican priest J. I. Packer if I could change the wording of the Absolution, the pronouns "we" to "I" and "our" to "my." I wondered if I could say the Absolution to myself. Was I forgiving myself? He looked at me very intently and answered my last question. "Not only should you say the Absolution, you must. You need to hear the words." Not being a priest, I pray the words of the more general Absolution: "Grant to your faithful people, merciful Lord, pardon and peace, that [I] may be cleansed from all [my] sins, and serve you with a quiet mind; through Jesus Christ our Lord. Amen."[11]

Just as Confession is always followed by the Absolution, the Absolution is always followed by praise. Just as God stands waiting to forgive in the Absolution, we stand to enjoy and celebrate His loving grace.

Our praise starts with the Invitatory (antiphonal singing some call the Suffrage), a moment to ask God to initiate our praise, to lead us into it. As we sing to God and one another, I know that as I need God to show me my sin, I also need help to praise Him. It doesn't come naturally. A member of the choir sings, "Glory be to the Father and to the Son and to the Holy Spirit" (how does she hit that high note every time?) and the congregation responds, singing, "As it was in the beginning, is now and ever shall be, world without end. Amen."

This morning we also express our praise in singing the Venite, Psalm 95. It's a giant "Come!"—celebrating the magnificence of the Absolution and welcoming the Scripture readings. Its words remind me of the "joy of our salvation," that we are given this tangible joy together.

Knowing whether to sing the Venite or the Jubilate for the Invitatory was one of the many reasons I was intimidated that first Sunday. How did anyone know? What I eventually learned was that the options in the prayer book were there to be steppingstones, to offer a path to deepen worship, to sink us into God's year and God's story. The crucial steppingstones are always Confession, Absolution, Scripture, and Prayer, with praise and sentences of Scripture tying these together. They are there to help us.

Thomas Cranmer, the archbishop of Canterbury who compiled the first Book of Common Prayer in 1542, was not only an esteemed literary scholar but a true pastor. He was a brilliant compiler and choreographer of worship. His heart was with his parishioners. He longed for people to know Christ's love in all things, and to know personally that we are held in God's story. He understood that such knowledge did not come easily. We needed steps to get there.

To support us, Cranmer placed the liturgical steppingstones in a progression, a pattern that I sensed in my first visit to the Anglican church but could not name—a progression of sin-grace-faith (others call it guilt-grace-gratitude). Like three movements in a piece of music, after several times through we start to feel the pattern. We begin to anticipate it. We sink into it more fully. In Morning and Evening Prayer we walk through the progression once; in the service of Holy Communion, twice. In every service, the Exhortation and Confession walk us through our sin. The Absolution and praise pull us into grace and Scripture. The Creed and the Prayers nudge us onward in faith. There is so much more going on in our worship than just the words we are saying.

Having sung God's praise, the congregation sits to hear the Scripture readings. There's another communal "thump" as everyone sits down: a thump that conveys a gladness, that we have completed something hefty. We have confessed to God and been thoroughly forgiven.

This morning an adorable nine-year-old girl with a long blond braid reads the Old Testament passage. She reads the verses as if they are fascinating, when in fact they are a long list of unpronounceable names. The congregation is clearly tempted to applaud when she reaches the end, and she looks up with a small smile. She was not just adorable, she was flawless. Two Sundays ago an elderly gentleman hobbled up the stairs to the lectern, his cane tapping on every step as we held our breath, worrying he might fall. He read the passages with the best of a David Attenborough inflection; I half wanted him to continue on about turtles and ancient forests. Last Sunday a tattooed graduate student read to us, his man-bun neatly pulled back and a big smile on his face. God's Word belongs to all of us.

The Bible readings are taken from a lengthy list found at the very back (or sometimes at the beginning) of the prayer book, organized by Sundays, by weeks of the Liturgical Year. Some versions call it the Lectionary, others call it the Table of Lessons. I used to wonder, "Why a reading from Numbers this week, and Zephaniah last week?" until someone pointed me to the Lectionary and explained its organization. Following these patterns of Scripture readings provides a structure to read through the whole of the Bible in three years (some prayer books also offer a structure to read through it in one year). These readings connect us with Christians around the world. They create a commonality.

We read the Lectionary passages in the company of those in Manhattan and those in Mombasa. Following the Lectionary puts us all on that river barge, seeing the vista of Scripture, of God's great story, together.

In the early months of Covid-19, I discovered the odd bonding of a common language. Walking our border collie, Finlay, I passed the same people walking their dogs almost every day, some of whom I'd seen for close to ten years. We knew each other by appearance and by our collies and poodles and retrievers, but never by name. We rarely did more than nod. But as we were locked down at home, our walks in the park resembled prisoners heading out to the yard, thrilled for fresh air and connection. We started talking. We felt the freedom to ask each other's names. We knew our questions were of the same language—How are you? Holding up okay? Anyone sick yet? We now knew we had something in common besides our dogs.

Reading the Lectionary's common readings has the same effect. We might not know each other, but together we are progressing through the shared language and story of Scripture.

⟡

In our church, the readings in Morning Prayer usually begin with the Psalms, their poetic effect settling upon us with their alternating between heartbreak ("Where are you, O Lord, when I need You?") and reassurance ("You have placed your love upon me"). They are exceptionally humane. The psalm is frequently followed by an Old Testament reading, or this morning in our church, preceded by it. The readings nearly always include a New Testament passage and a reading from one of the four Gospels.

After the readings, we pause to greet one another—a quick hello to those sitting in the same pew. The greeting seems to mark another turning point. In saying good morning to each other, some we know and some we don't, we acknowledge we are doing this odd, counter-cultural process together—we are worshiping God.

Some congregations respond to the Scripture readings with a Canticle, singing the Benedictus or the Te Deum, both sung prayers of praise that highlight the goodness of the Lord and the goodness and gift of His Word. Like the Lectionary readings, these responses remind me that we are rejoicing with a vast range of worshipers—the church across that world.

This praise is followed by the Apostles' Creed, and I am often struck by the many ways the Creed reiterates the praise we have just sung. The Apostles' Creed tells our story, the one we fling or ease ourselves into as people in Christ.

We stand to say it. The Apostles' Creed is my home page—or at least, that's what I want it to be. Instead of living in the domain of world powers, Instagram, and worries about my kids and the planet, saying the Creed situates me in God's foundation and in His certain hope. I am comforted that for nearly two thousand years, millions of saints and sinners, known and unknown, have lived their lives based on the Creed's realities rather than their circumstances.

Out of the corner of my eye I see the Marstons, one row behind me and over to my left. In their early fifties, tall, neatly dressed with carefully combed hair, they stand together. She's an English teacher and he's an engineer. They look composed, but her face gives me clues that all is not easy, and I wonder if that pain comes from marriage or poor health. She says the Creed with her eyes closed, as if she's sinking deep into all that it means to say those words, to choose their ways. I love her earnestness. He says them like he's taking an oath in a courtroom, like he's making a choice that does not come naturally. I value his recognition that the Creed presents you with a decision, one you have to make each week, each morning.

Our congregation seems to have grasped that we need to say the Creed together. We start slowly to get in sync. We listen for each other. We say the sentences carefully because these truths were given, not earned, and because they are life-giving. God could have abandoned us. Christ could have avoided the cross. The Holy Spirit could have chosen to leave us. But because God is the God of all mercies, none of these things happened, or could happen. This isn't a chant at the end of the huddle. Because the Creed is true, all will be well.

Following the Scriptures and the Creed, we sit for the sermon, most frequently a time of teaching that expounds one of the readings. Some days I listen better than others.

Following the teaching, we kneel to pray for all that is on our hearts and in our minds. It's a rare day that I don't ask God for a lot. We started the morning's service by remembering who Christ is and who we are in Him, and now we bring the specifics of our lives and world to place into His hands. As we have moved from acknowledging our sin to receiving His grace, now we ask—in faith.

We begin with the Lord's Prayer. We kneel (more scuffing and thumps) to pray to our Father, who stays awake while we sleep, who waits for us to pray again, who loved us before the world began. I remind myself as I pray that God is personal. It seems so impossible.

The collects come next. Collects are short prayers that often express what we have heard in the readings, concerns we have in common. They are full of treasured cadences like "who wonderfully created, and yet more wonderfully restored, the dignity of human nature," or "whose property is always to have mercy."

We conclude with the Collect for Grace:

O LORD our heavenly Father, Almighty and everlasting God, who hast safely brought us to the beginning of this day: Defend us in the same with thy mighty power; and grant that this day we fall into no sin, neither run into any kind of danger; but that all our doings may be ordered by thy governance, to do always that is righteous in thy sight; through Jesus Christ our Lord. Amen.[12]

At the end of these prayers, we are led in the Intercessions by someone from our congregation. Here we pray more specifically—for the homeless and poor of our cities, for our government leaders, for those in violent conflict or terrible disasters, for those fighting wildfires, for medical staff in remote countries, for the people of Ukraine, for those who are sick in our own congregation. We end with a time of silence in which we ask for God's care for our own concerns. Today it's my son who's struggling to get a decent job, my aging mother, a meeting Monday morning that is apt to be contentious, my husband's hip pain that's keeping him from cycling.

Concluding our prayer time, we end with a giant thank-you in the Great Thanksgiving. It's the quintessential omnibus prayer.

ALMIGHTY God, Father of all mercies, We thine unworthy servants do give thee most humble and hearty thanks For all thy goodness and loving-kindness, To us and to all people. We bless thee for our creation, preservation, and all the blessings of this life; But above all for thine inestimable love in the redemption of the world by our Lord Jesus Christ; For the means of grace, And for the hope of glory. And we beseech thee, give us that due sense of all thy mercies, That our hearts may be unfeignedly thankful, And that we show forth thy praise, Not only with our lips, but in our lives; By giving up ourselves to thy service, And by walking before thee in holiness and righteousness all our days; Through Jesus Christ our Lord, To whom, with thee and the Holy Ghost, be all honour and glory, world without end. Amen.[13]

I love the seven "alls" (as one poet describes them, "all the alls")— they expand within me as we say them—*all* goodness, *all* people, *all* blessings, *all* mercies, *all* days.

At its core, we are saying thanks for our salvation in Christ, for loving us so much, "for thine inestimable love in the redemption of the world by our Lord Jesus Christ." It's a prayer that embodies its substance.

Literary scholar Alan Jacobs writes, "For many who have felt themselves at the mercy of chaotic forces from within or without, the style of the prayer book has healing powers. It provides equitable balance when we ourselves have none."[14]

I think of Jacobs's words when people ask me about the repetition in using the prayer book. I know that I learn through repetition, and this has gotten truer as I get older. To repeat something to myself is often the beginning of internalizing it, for good and for ill.

When one of our sons was twelve or thirteen, he complained because he wanted to go to a church with more spontaneity. Why did our church have to be so formal, to say fancy words over and over? One of the things I remember him saying was, "I could be shaped by any old words I say week after week; it wouldn't matter if it was a beer commercial!"

I thought a lot about this. I tried reciting a few beer commercials several days in a row. "You only go around once in this life, so you have to grab for all the gusto you can get"[15] and "Head for the mountains"[16] were two I experimented on. "If you've got the time, we've got the beer"[17] didn't do much. What I eventually figured out was that for words to stay with you, to shape you, they need resonance, to get traction in our tender hearts—and beer commercials don't reach that standard. The prayer book, so deeply saturated with Scripture, does.

The Prayer of Thanksgiving is followed by the short prayer of Saint John Chrysostom, and then the blessing, my favorite of which is from Saint Paul's letter to the Philippians, "And the peace of God, which transcends all understanding, will guard your hearts and your minds in Christ Jesus" (Philippians 4:7).

Our worship service ends with more music, usually a hymn and postlude. In the music we are given the chance to tuck ourselves into the goodness and truths of our worship, a sustenance for the week ahead.

At the very close, after we are sure the last notes of the postlude have truly ended, there is a fun sort of mayhem—shuffling and grabbing of coats but also a move toward coffee (and hopefully doughnuts) in the big common room behind the sanctuary. Kids who were in Sunday school find their parents and race off again to snacks. We chat, introduce ourselves more fully to someone near us we don't know, get a hug from a friend. The tone at the end is so different than at the beginning. As Tim Challies hoped, in the Call to Worship "we have been reminded who we really are, reminded who Christ is."

⚜

I had only participated in the service of Evening Prayer once or twice, but as Covid-19 clamped down on us in March 2020, Evening Prayer changed our lives as well.

Two of our kids had decided to come back to Vancouver, one from Los Angeles and one from Montreal. They were both isolated and lonely. Craig and I tossed them the keys to our second car at the airport so they could quarantine at our house for two weeks, and we headed to our small cottage in the islands to wait them out. Within the next ten days, as the world changed, our doctor said to us, "Stay put. Don't leave the island; don't go anywhere. The kids are together in your house. They're fine."

Old friends just up the driveway were also staying put. In our isolation, the four of us began to have Evening Prayer on our deck. Every night, rain or shine, at 5:00 p.m. we'd finish whatever we were doing, shut down our laptops, and grab our jackets (and occasionally our blankets). Our friends would arrive and we'd debrief about the day, share global and local news, and then begin to pray.

To say that Evening Prayer was a lifeline would be an understatement. Our friends were often the only people we saw in a day or a week. We took turns reading the psalm, Old Testament, and New Testament passages aloud and saying the liturgy together.

Usually the four of us sang a hymn. "I Feel the Winds of God Today" was our favorite, and remembering our happy but off-key voices singing to the waves crashing in the Salish Sea—"If cast on shores of selfish ease, or pleasure I should be, O let me feel your freshening breeze, and I'll put back to sea"[18]—cheers me still. It makes me teary too.

Saying Evening Prayer so regularly gave us all a new adventure and a road home. Its words tethered us to each other, to hope for the days ahead, to Christ. For nearly twelve weeks, this liturgy was our perch.

Evening Prayer differs slightly from Morning Prayer in content but not structure. It is intended to be said as evening begins, ideally right before dinner, and it follows the same progression of sin-grace-faith, moving from the Opening Sentences to General Confession and Absolution to Scripture readings and the Creed; collects to closing blessing. It, too, is a dialogue with God. If you are in a church setting, there are wonderful sung pieces interspersed that suit the closing of the daytime hours. Evening Prayer is shorter than Morning Prayer, and it reflects the vulnerability of the darkness ahead (and in our case, the pandemic around us). It asks, "by your great mercy defend us from all perils and dangers of this night." We entreat the Lord that "your holy angels may lead us in paths of peace and goodwill."[19]

Created long before there was electricity to keep us at work and up later at night, Evening Prayer shifts us to face our vulnerability, our need to rest in Christ. While in Morning Prayer we pray for the vulnerability of the day and possible dangers ahead, in Evening Prayer we focus on God's protection, on His holding us secure. We say the words of Psalm 139, "'Surely the darkness shall cover me,' then shall my night be turned to day. Even the darkness is not dark to you, and the night is as clear as the day; the darkness and the light to you are both alike" (Psalm 139:10-11).

We confess, we are forgiven, we hear His Word, we ask for His care upon our lives, we give thanks. We walk the steps through a less obvious but far more accurate and hopeful story of our world and our lives. Darkness remains and so does our vulnerability, but lightened and reminded of God's strength and unswerving presence, we are ready to rest in the assurances of Evening Prayer.

It was and is a lovely way to end the day.

2

The COLLECTS

*O*hhh . . . It's not here."

"What's not here?"

Early on a Monday morning I was grabbing a mug of tea to take upstairs when Lisa poked her head into the kitchen. She was our favorite of the runners who helped with Finlay's insatiable need for exercise. Her cheeks and nose were red with cold, and I wondered if what she was missing was a jacket she could borrow.

"That poem—or is it a prayer?" she said. "The one about 'being brought to this day,' and 'not running into danger.' It's usually on the little bulletin board above the dog food. I'm not religious at all but I always like seeing it. It's weirdly comforting. I was looking forward to it this morning. Did someone take it?"

Nearly ten years ago Craig had taped up a copy of the Collect for Grace, the same prayer we say at the close of Morning Prayer, by our back door. I'm guessing he meant it to be a sort of a benediction as we all raced in and out of the house.

On what had become a torn and splattered (and now missing) piece of paper, the prayer read:

Almighty and everlasting God, who hast safely brought us to the
beginning of this day: Defend us in the same with thy mighty
power; and grant that this day we fall into no sin, neither run
into any kind of danger; but that all our doings may be ordered
by thy governance, to do always that is righteous in thy sight;
through Jesus Christ our Lord. Amen.[1]

Like haiku or sonnets in poetry, collects (pronounced with the em-
phasis on the first syllable—COL-lects) are a particular form of prayers.
Their content varies widely but their shape stays roughly the same.
They are called *collects* because they "collect" the voices of the people.
There are more than 150 of them in the Anglican Book of Common
Prayer. There are collects for the sick, the anxious, the grateful; for an
election, for natural disasters, for farming. There are collects for those
going to sea, those who work in hospitals, and those starting school.
There is one for every week of the year and every saint's day, and they
are woven in throughout the services of Morning Prayer, Holy
Communion, Baptisms, Weddings, funerals, and more.

Four to nine lines long (and wonderfully terse), collects usually
include five ingredients, in this order: (1) an address to God, (2) an
acknowledgment or attribute of who God is, (3) a request, (4) a
reason for our asking, and (5) a reason why we can ask God for this.
Collects are what church historian Bruce Hindmarsh often describes as "contritional and aspirational." They often include
lament for our sin with phrases such as "all hearts open, all desires
known," and "no health in us," but they also seek what's truly
good—"that we may perfectly love thee" or "that all our doings may
be ordered by their governance."

Most of these prayers are so old it's impossible to know who wrote
them. Historians date some of them back to the eighth century
Eucharist services of the Western liturgy. Other collects were composed in the sixteenth century, during the Protestant Reformation.

Thomas Cranmer chose many of them from earlier sources, but he also wrote a number of the favorites himself.

The collect by our back door comes near the end of the service of Morning Prayer. On the days I notice it as I head out, it reminds me again of one of my favorite pieces of art, the Henry Ossawa Tanner painting *The Good Shepherd*.[2] It shows a shepherd carrying one of his young sheep down a steep, rocky mountainside. Saddled over the shepherd's shoulders, the lamb looks curious and content, so confident in her rescuer that her legs hang relaxed over his left shoulder as she ponders the landscape. Collects, like the shepherd, have a way of reaching down into the anxious part of me that asks, "Can I handle all this?"—one of many worries I shove down deep—and pulling me close to God's care.

A friend once said to me that the Collect for Grace made her feel cared for, not as a competent person, but as a nervous, insecure child, and in experiencing that tender care, she began to learn to rest in God.

Collects don't just show us what we can pray for, they knit us together. They gather our worries and longings and hopes, and they gather us. When I say the Collect for Grace, the words "brought us" and "defend us" remind me that we all long to be carried on God's shoulders; we all want God to do the defending. I'm not the only one. With this collect being more than a thousand years old, I know that people have been articulating these longings for a very long time. In saying the "we," I nestle into the community of pilgrims. We all arrived at this day "safely brought," even before we hopped on the bus or arrived at work.

On the same morning Lisa missed the Collect for Grace, I got to my office in the loft of our house, despaired at my messy piles atop my long wooden desk, took a deep breath in hopes of clearing my mind of the minutiae, and made myself pray.

I started by asking for forgiveness for being snarky toward my son (I did want him to empty the dishwasher, but I didn't ask him well). Then I prayed for the work I was about to do:

> O LORD, who hast taught us that all our doings without charity are nothing worth: Send thy Holy Spirit, and pour into our hearts that most excellent gift of charity, the very bond of peace and all virtues, without which whosoever liveth is counted dead before thee. Grant this for thine only Son Jesus Christ's sake. Amen.[3]

Although this collect echoes 1 Corinthians 13 (which many have heard and read countless times), it first got my attention one morning in church when I was fishing around in my leather bag beneath our pew, panicked that I needed to answer a text. It needed a quick response and I was afraid I'd forget. I rarely text midservice but Craig gave me the "What are you doing?" grimace—and just as he did so, the congregation said this collect.

The connection between texting in church and worshiping without love was too close for comfort. I was trying to worship efficiently, to love God efficiently. But efficiency and worship (not to mention love) are much better when they're kept apart.

This collect soon became my "Before I Start Working" prayer. I say it most mornings. The words offer me a fresh reminder that God doesn't want my priority to be getting more done. He cares more how I do things than what I do. Jesus didn't worry about efficiency or punctuality in his life on earth, and He still doesn't. Whether I am editing a document, sitting in a Zoom meeting, or making spinach lasagna, God wants me to do what I do with love. As it was for the Good Samaritan, love is more important than punctuality.

My "Before I Start to Work" prayer is only four lines long, but it quotes or echoes twenty-eight different verses of Scripture. On the days I am rushed (or efficient), the collects drizzle God's words into me; they infuse my prayers with God's wisdom rather than my own concerns.

J. I. Packer frequently explained that the prayer book was the "Bible arranged for worship."[4] More than 75 percent of its words (some would say 80 percent) are taken directly from Scripture. Reading its services, letting its words sink in, memorizing it by praying it day after day does not compete with Scripture but puts it in a form that sticks. I no longer feel embarrassed that I know far more of the Book of Common Prayer from memory than I do of Scripture.

❦

Tuesday afternoon I went to be with our friend Everett at his hospital bed—his wife had a long day and she wanted someone to be with him. Everett was dying of heart failure. I had no clue what to say or do. I wasn't sure if he would know I was there. Should I take chocolate, a *New York Times*, a flask of good whiskey? Was there any point in bringing anything? I sat quietly for a bit, but after a while, still not knowing what to say, I said I wanted to pray for him. Did he nod or was that just a twitch?

I pulled my Book of Common Prayer out of my bag, got on my knees, and read the Collect for the Sick: "God of all grace and power: Behold, visit, and relieve this thy servant; look upon him with the eyes of thy mercy, give him comfort and sure confidence in thee, defend him in all danger, and keep him in perpetual peace and safety; through Jesus Christ our Lord. Amen."[5]

Hearing it aloud, I was a bit stunned. How could that short seven-hundred-year-old prayer be so pertinent to the precariousness of Ev's life in a huge, sophisticated hospital? In far better language than I could have conjured up, the collect named what I didn't know I wanted so badly—that God would behold him, that he would feel known and comforted and kept in peace. I would have prayed for him to be healed, cared for by the good doctors, to know his kids' love—but for God to "behold" him? That was far more tending than I could have cobbled together on my own.

By naming an essential aspect of God's character—"of all grace and power," or "who safely brought us to the beginning of this day"—the collects nudge me to see who God is, showing me again that God is always waiting for me, for each of us, and that He's waiting to lavish us with grace. He never stops waiting, never leaves us without a ride home. These short descriptions push back at the whispers that tell me that there is no God, or worse, that He doesn't care, and that because He doesn't care, I can't trust Him. The collects vivify God's loving character and constancy, His reliability.

I wondered if Everett gave me the slightest of raised eyebrows when I looked up from praying; maybe he, too, was surprised at the goodness of being beheld.

Wednesday was mundane with work, groceries, a meal delivered to my friend. Mary is in her nineties and several of us bring meals and little bouquets and pray with her. As I headed back to my car, I thought of the collect (usually called the Prayer of Saint Chrysostom) that comes to mind when several of us band together to pray.

> ALMIGHTY God, who hast given us grace at this time with one accord to make our common supplications unto thee; and dost promise that when two or three are gathered together in thy Name thou wilt grant their requests: Fulfil now O Lord, the desires and petitions of thy servants, as may be most expedient for them; granting us in this world knowledge of thy truth, and in the world to come life everlasting. Amen.[6]

I am always struck by the phrase "granting us in this world knowledge of thy truth," placed immediately after we have asked for our desires and petitions to be granted, "as may be most expedient for them." Seeing which of our desires are "expedient" (and those that are not) seems to require a God-given wisdom and grace, and usually time. Mary is old enough to know death is close, and I can see that what she wants, even more than healing, is to know we are with her, that God is with her, that she's not alone. I wish I had raced back to her door for a second wave.

Thursday was similar: a deadline to meet, a long (and expensive) call with my mother's accountant. The violence in Baghdad loomed in my mind. It is difficult to imagine how hard it must be for the people living in the constancy and horror of turmoil. I was in bed by nine, grateful for the quiet of my neighborhood and my country, and the pleasure of my novel. The Collect for Eventide was all I could muster.

O Lord, support us all the day long through this trouble-filled life, until the shadows lengthen, and the evening comes, and the busy world is hushed, the fever of life is over, and our work is done. Then in your mercy grant us a safe lodging, and a holy rest, and peace at the last. Amen.[7]

I wanted that safe lodging for the people of Baghdad, for the people of Ukraine, that they, too, would enjoy holy rest and peace, now and at the last.

On Friday afternoon I went to a very chilly, windy ground-breaking ceremony for a small chapel at the university not far from my family's house. Why they were holding this event in late November I wasn't quite sure, but a treasured older friend had left the instructions and money for the chapel to be built in his will, and his family invited me to the occasion. I was honored to be asked, and annoyed at having to give up an afternoon. The university's president and a few faculty, decked in flapping academic robes, traipsed in before us, a bagpiper serenading them onto the little stage. The president, glasses low on his nose, grayish hair ruffling in the wind, looked tentative. He began by looking down at his notes and shrugging his shoulders as if he was going to apologize, and then he spoke to the small group.

"I feel like a fraud today as I am not usually the one to preside over future buildings that will take on a religious role. But as we were processing in just now, I remembered a prayer that I heard as a child growing up in the Episcopal Church. I think it was in the service of Evening Prayer. I am shocked both that I remember it"—he paused and smiled sheepishly—"and how fitting it is: 'Visit, this place, O Lord, and drive far from it all snares of the enemy; let your holy angels dwell with us to preserve us in peace; and let your blessing be upon us always; through Jesus Christ our Lord. Amen.'"[8]

The president stopped speaking suddenly, and the audience realized he'd teared up. He looked stunned. My guess was that this short Collect for Protection came back to him after forty years, and yet its relevance in this setting left him speechless. I sensed that he found himself genuinely wanting God's blessing "to be always upon" this future building and the people using it to be "in peace." The twenty or thirty of us there that day will probably never forget the moment— and I am fairly certain it was exactly what my friend who gave the chapel hoped it might be.

I am guessing, too, that the university president remembered the prayer in part because of its rhythm and brevity. Most of the collects were written with a poet's use of repetition and alliteration, skillfully placed in a pattern of heavily and lightly accented syllables. If we say the collects week after week, they will still be there forty years later. The next line just comes. I said collects long before I realized they were prayers united by a specific form, that even though they differed in content, they had a similarity. I'm quite sure it was their rhythm that kept them easy to pull up.

Their brilliance shines in their brevity too. I show up gladly for church most Sundays, but when someone prays "off the cuff" I notice they can go on too long, they can stuff in too much. There's a tendency to posture, to preach even within the prayers. I can absorb the collects' intentions into my mind and heart more easily, each with its one

request—defend, protect, cleanse, comfort, lighten, bless. I've got
room for them.

⚬⚬✦⚬⚬

On Saturday night shortly before I headed up to bed, I texted my
sister my "Night Time Collect." A few years ago she'd had a myste-
rious illness, and living alone became terrifying. She worried about
being found dead on her floor; I worried about her lying there with
no one to call the ambulance. To deal with our worries, we began a
system of texting each other morning and evening.

My sister often sends me several texts each day, some two and three
inches long. I rarely send more than two, and mine are two to three
lines long. But wanting to be supportive, I began texting her a collect
before I went to bed. She's taken to sending me one right back. Our
favorite is:

> O LORD, who hast pity for all our weakness: Put away from us
> worry and every anxious fear, that, having ended the labours of
> the day as in thy sight, and committing our tasks, ourselves, and
> all we love into thy keeping, we may, now that night cometh,
> receive as from thee thy priceless gift of sleep; through Jesus
> Christ our Lord. Amen.[9]

Taken from the ancient version of the evening Compline service,
this prayer is called the Collect for the Freedom from Worry, and while
I may not be a champion texter, I am a champion worrier. That
Saturday night I was struck again by the consolation I found in seeing
that God pities (which in this context means "lavishes compassion
upon") not just my worries, but my worrying. God wants to hold my
aches and concerns so I can enjoy sleep.

⚬⚬✦⚬⚬

On any Sunday morning our church's Holy Communion service
could have as many as six collects or as few as three, but the Collect

for Purity is always where we start. It's our reset as we return to worship and I'm always glad it's waiting for me. I need resets.

> ALMIGHTY God, unto whom all hearts be open, all desires known, and from whom no secrets are hid: Cleanse the thoughts of our hearts by the inspiration of thy Holy Spirit, that we may perfectly love thee, and worthily magnify thy holy Name; through Christ our Lord. Amen.[10]

The beginning to this collect (the acknowledgment of who God is), "unto whom all hearts be open, all desires known, and from whom no secrets are hid," feels odd in the twenty-first century. Its words acknowledge that He knows we have sinned, that we try to hide parts of ourselves, often in shame, and that He longs to come into our hearts and minds to cleanse and unburden us—and to do so by His inspiration, not our efforts. God never asks us to clean ourselves; he asks for permission that we might be open to Him doing the cleaning. He says to me, let my Spirit declutter, vacuum in the crevices.

Some mornings what I love best is that we ask for this cleansing together. Side by side on our knees, I hear friends and strangers, relief and longing in their voices, wanting to be free of their facades and longing for that amazing grace as we begin to worship yet again.

This morning was the first Sunday in Advent. Because of this time of waiting in the church calendar, the sanctuary was more drab than usual. The only color poking out was the long, narrow purple banners lining the front of the altar and the green Advent wreath, with its four pristine candles poised to be lit by an eager child. Advent means "coming," and it's the practice of waiting for Christ's coming, which we do in the four weeks before Christmas. As novelist Frederick Buechner writes, "Advent is like the hush in a theater just before the curtain rises."[11]

As the liturgical calendar sets Scripture readings for each week, there is also the set collect, and not long after we knelt to say the opening Collect for Purity, we knelt again to pray the Collect for the first Sunday in Advent.

> Almighty God, give us grace to cast away the works of darkness, and put on the armor of light, now in the time of this mortal life in which your Son Jesus Christ came to visit us in great humility; that in the last day, when he shall come again in his glorious majesty to judge both the living and the dead, we may rise to the life immortal; through him who lives and reigns with you and the Holy Spirit, one God, now and for ever. Amen.[12]

Vancouver, in the southwest corner of Canada, is geographically one of the world's best places to move through the church year. Our climate and seasons echo the darkness and light perfectly. As Advent begins in late November, the darkness falls on us by 4:00 p.m. and lasts until 8:00 in the morning. Our measly eight hours of daylight limit what we do, and what we don't do—when we walk the dog, when we meet for a soccer game, when we rake up the endless autumn leaves.

This morning I longed for the armor of light to get me through these short days, through the unending disappointments and disruptions, through the recent deaths of three friends.

But in my longing, I noticed something I had missed last Advent. These contrasts—cast off darkness/put on light, now/in the last day, mortal life/life immortal, great humility/glorious majesty—are all connected by the "now." As the Collect for the first Sunday in Advent puts it, "now in the time of this mortal life." God is not just holding the opposing realities; God is holding the dichotomies. In the collects I learn that God is holding my falling and His defending, my danger and His beholding, the lengthening shadows and holy rest, the enemies and the peace, the worries and the priceless gift of sleep. He is shedding light into these things even now. He isn't eliminating them, but He gives me an armor of light to wear through them, even in the darkest and coldest days of the year.

Collects show me the way. They are my prayers and my teachers in prayer. Together with those before me and those across the planet, they show that it's God who brought us safely to the beginning of this day, who gives comfort and sure confidence, who gives safe lodging, and at the last, a perfect end. The collects are my candles, my flashlights in the darkness, pointing to God's great and personal love amid the tensions, and the darkness, always in great humility.

3

PRAYERS *for* FAMILIES
and INDIVIDUALS

We get up early. Craig and I both like that alcove of time when the world feels still and we can wake up slowly. As we get our tea and coffee, I mumble, "Sleep okay?" Craig worries aloud that we are out of cream (we aren't). Wrapped in our flannel robes, we sink into our spots in the sitting area off our kitchen, me in the red armchair and Craig on the slouchy couch. Daylight and caffeine slowly settle on us. Our cell phones stay face down on the counter. Finlay sits at my feet, antsy for his walk.

But then—and not because we feel like it—we put down our mugs and pray.

If we had to come up with the words to pray early in the morning, we wouldn't pray at all. We're not that disciplined; we don't want to get in each other's way. Craig's too quiet. I care too much about getting the words right, and remembering everyone I said I'd pray for. We are both too weary. He wants to ride his bike, and I want to get out with the dog so I can get to work.

Saying the prayer book's Family Prayer began as a solution. This very short service offered a way for Craig and me to pray together without organizing ourselves, without emotional inclination. These prayers are not an abridged version of Morning Prayer but they are scriptural and theologically wise.

We need both.

Craig knows the eight short prayers of this liturgy from memory. He said to me once that having memorized them has made space for the Holy Spirit to enter in, to speak to him, that with a foundation there is more room, not less.

I like the prayer book in my hands. I find seeing the words a comfort, a tangible confirmation these enduring prayers are still here. Last sips of coffee gulped down, the dog shifting around eager to make sure I know he's ready to go, we start with two lines of the Psalms, early verses of Psalm 63 and Psalm 5.

"O God, you are my God; early will I seek thee. Early in the morning will I direct my prayer unto you, and will look up."

Some of the first prayers for early morning were written for monks, starting their day of worship in the darkness before the dawn, literally asking God to be the One to open their lips at the beginning of the day. I envision them in their long brown robes, snow falling quietly outside their walls, as weary as Craig and I but glad their first words of the day could bring their minds back to God, speaking to Him before speaking to each other.

At least as much as the monks, I need a way to begin my day looking to God, addressing Him before I face the world around me. Already feeling the gravitational pull of my day, I need the prayer book as a way of remembering and reorienting that we live in God's world, God's love, God's story.

After these opening lines, we say the Lord's Prayer. Even if I am saying it alone, even if one of our sons or a houseguest is in the kitchen making coffee, I make myself say it aloud (quietly), to make it mine and to hear it fall upon me. I try to concentrate on each line, to fight the distraction of wondering whether there's bread for the person in the kitchen, or who might have texted me this morning. What temptations might be in store this day? Mine are usually a lie to cover up a mistake, an attempt to make myself look more generous or skillful than I am. I try to slow down my words enough to think through my petitions, to pray a prayer within the prayer that God will show me which temptations might be waiting, or who I need to forgive.

A crucial part of the Lord's Prayer for me is the last line, "For yours is the kingdom and the power and the glory forever." While these closing words are not part of the Lord's Prayer in some manuscripts of the Bible, they call me back to seeing that the world—the kingdom of God, the planet, North America, my back-alley neighbors, my family—is all God's. Again, it's help for remembering.

❧❧❧

One Sunday morning after our church service had ended, I was chatting with friends and Craig was trying to be patient but was eager to be off. He was hungry for lunch and looking forward to a football game. Sitting in a back pew, looking so focused that he repelled interruption, Craig flipped through the small red prayer book (our pew prayer books are the 1962 Canadian version) and noticed the Family Prayers tucked in at the very end, nestled so far in the back of the book that he probably wondered why they were included at all.

Craig and I had talked countless times about praying together regularly, but in more than twenty years of dating and marriage, we'd never done it.[1] We loved the concept of saying the services of Morning and Evening Prayer daily, ideally with our kids, but we couldn't make it happen. Our schedules were too different. We prayed together in a crisis, but even then, it was a struggle. Craig told me once that one of the things that made it hard to pray with me was the surprise. Midprayer I would add something like, "May my biopsy go easily tomorrow; may the results be good." Craig would wonder, "What? You have another biopsy tomorrow? Why am I finding this out now?"

With no possibility for surprises or long petitions, Craig suggested we give these prayers a try first thing in the morning. Since the Sunday he found them, we have said these together at least several mornings a week. Despite their name, I have never once prayed them with my kids.

❧❧❧❧

After the Lord's Prayer, we give thanks and ask for God's help. "We give thee hearty thanks, oh heavenly Father, for the rest of the past night and the gift of a new day. Grant that we may so pass its hours in the perfect freedom of thy service that at eventide we may again give thanks unto thee; through Jesus Christ our Lord."[2]

For the third time in two minutes, I see that life, all of life, and the world that holds it all, is a gift of God: the sleep I've had in a quiet night and warm house, the sun that's risen, and the safety I've taken for granted. Even a modicum of predictability in the sunrise and the safety of my neighborhood are gifts.

The phrase "perfect freedom of thy service" initially felt like a biblical oxymoron. Service that brings satisfaction, or even personal growth, maybe. But freedom? Perfect freedom? The truth can set us free, but can service? I lose sight of the reality that while I am certainly not a slave to my employer, I am a slave to wanting respect, to making money, and of course, to my phone and email. In the sixteen hours of my day, I focus far more on appeasing these entities than I focus on serving God. Forgetting my freedom, I lapse into becoming the Prodigal Son's older brother, expecting God to treat me well if I'm well-behaved. I fall into being transactional so easily.

Remembering my similarity to the Prodigal Son's older brother and thinking about the apostle Paul's words to the Galatians about freedom sprinkled into this prayer of thanks, I see that these prayers are constantly scriptural. The prayer book offers me Scripture before I even open my Bible (and even when I don't).

This short collection of prayers, Family Prayer, has an odd history.[3] The prayers were not originally in the prayer book. Cranmer's hope was that everyone—children, employees, parents—would gather for the full Morning and Evening Prayers; they would stop their tasks, ideally with a priest in their presence, and pray. He saw no need for a shorter version.

But in 1705, Edmund Gibson, a Latin scholar and highly respected rector of Lambeth (and later bishop of London), wrote a lovely letter and treatise to his "Parish of Lambeth and Its Inhabitants"—an "Exhortation to Family Prayer."[4] Despite having eleven children, and despite addressing his Exhortation to families, he stated unequivocally that he wrote his treatise and prayers for everyone—those alone, those who could not get to a church without assistance, those who could not leave their work, even children on their own away from home.

With a lengthy wig of ringlets, long nose, and kind eyes, Gibson was even more a friend and pastor than he was an Oxford don. He began his Exhortation with a letter empathetically encouraging his parishioners to pray: "This exercise of Morning and Evening Prayer where Families have lived in the neglect of it, may appear somewhat strange at the Beginning, as all things do that are new and unusual."[5] He went on to explain why these prayers bring us to Christ—they bring us to receive God's love and kindness and presence. Even in his antiquated Georgian language, Gibson promised the prayers would be so short, "that the longer of them may be decently read in a little more than half a quarter of an Hour."[6] He separated the prayers into parts "so that we might avoid distraction."

I know those distractions well. Craig does too.

When the first American Book of Common Prayer was printed in 1789, Gibson was unknown in the States (and had passed away forty-one years earlier), but his prayers were added into the American

Prayer Book following the service of Compline. It was only in the twentieth century that this short service was added into other prayer book revisions, again placed after the service of Evening Prayer or Compline.

Canadians, wanting their own version of the prayer book in 1918, enlisted two bishops to write their own Families and Individuals Prayers. This liturgy was then slightly revised for the 1962 version, and while it has had little traction elsewhere, it remains my favorite— and the version Craig and I continue to use.

~⧫⧫⧫~

After we express our thanks and ask for that unusual-but-life-giving freedom, the prayer book suggests we read the Collect for the Day, the one assigned for that week of the Liturgical Year (and the same one we said in church on the previous Sunday).

This morning Craig had to leave very early so I read the Collect for the fourth Sunday after Epiphany by myself. It's one I look forward to, mostly for the word *upright*.

O GOD, who knowest us to be set in the midst of so many and great dangers, that by reason of the frailty of our nature we cannot always stand upright: Grant to us such strength and protection, as may support us in all dangers, and carry us through all temptations; through Jesus Christ our Lord. Amen.[7]

My day does not feel endangered with threats of gunfire or hurricanes, but the need to stand upright—staying wise and clear-minded in the midst of two meetings I have that morning and, equally hard, standing in the midst of cultural battles over politics, racism, and sexuality—feels precarious and personal. I struggle to stand upright not physically, but inwardly.

After the Collect for that week comes the Intercession, a prayer that contains one of the best sentences, and the best news, in all of the

Canadian prayer book. We have been awakened this day for two reasons—to praise God for His goodness and to ask for His grace. Every morning I'm relieved to hear these words, to know it's still true, to know it's all I am called to that day.

> O LORD God, who hast bidden light to shine out of darkness, and who hast again wakened us to praise thee for thy goodness and to ask for thy grace: Accept now the offering of our worship and thanksgiving, and grant unto us all such requests as may be acceptable to thy holy will. Make us to live as children of the light, and heirs of thy everlasting kingdom. Remember, O Lord, according to the multitude of thy mercies, thy whole Church, all who join with us in prayer, and all our brethren, wherever they may be, who stand in need of thine aid. Pour down upon us all the riches of thy grace, so that, redeemed in soul and body, and stedfast in faith, we may ever praise thy wonderful and holy Name; through Jesus Christ our Lord. Amen.[8]

"Bidden" pushes back at my tendency to think of God as manager rather than coaxer, the One who calls forth, the One who sees all the places of darkness and beckons light out of them. "Pour down upon us all the riches of thy grace" is a wonderful line; there is no tentativeness—no request for a standard-size container. Pour your life-giving grace all over us; soak and saturate us. Do the work for us, oh God.

These forthright verbs are favorites too—"accept, make, remember, pour." Pulled from the Psalms, they remind me how much we are encouraged to ask of God. It's one of the few places I am glad for the absence of a "please."

After the Intercession, Craig and I pray for our kids, for those we are worried about, for each other, for a friend who has to find a new place to live, for one of Craig's students who is having twins, for our city, for Canada, for America. We keep these requests short (with no surprises). Craig's prayers for me feel like love even when he's sleepy and grumpy. Hearing each other speak to God makes us more tender-hearted toward each other, and to our days.

The dog moves again in his restlessness. Buses honk as they speed by our house; the daylight starts to brighten the room. We end our requests with the Collect for Grace—our own addition but one that feels appropriate, and that comforts me as I hear it aloud.

The very last prayer praises the Trinity.

O GOD, Most High and Holy, Three in One,
Father, Son, and Holy Spirit: we offer to thee this day ourselves, our souls and bodies, to be a reasonable, holy, and living sac-rifice unto thee; to whom be all praise and glory. Amen.[9]

This offering echoes the prayer we say at Holy Communion, and I like the connection to Christ's offering for us as I begin the day. These words—yet more Scripture—restate part of Romans 12:1, pleading that our daily lives would be a form of worship, that we would give our day, our work, our intentions, even our hurrying off, to be folded into his bidding of light, to be what a friend calls "glimpses of hope" in our messy world. Mine feels like a fledgling sacrifice, and I'm glad for the word *reasonable*, which acknowledges that we can help, but not save, the world.

We close by saying the Grace, taken nearly verbatim from the very end of Paul's second letter to the church in Corinth, looking to God who we have been conversing with, and to each member of the Trinity. Paul doesn't ask the Father, Son, and Holy Spirit to be with us; he asks for blessings of the Trinity—grace, love, and fellowship—to be with us. "The grace of our Lord Jesus Christ, and the love of God, and the fel-lowship of the Holy Ghost be with us all, evermore."[10]

Finlay knows the cadence of the Grace so well that he pops up just as we say "Amen."

Saying the Morning Prayer for Families takes about five minutes. Gibson was right.

Every so often someone asks me how I use the prayer book in my prayers at home. If they are feeling comfortable, they usually also ask if I get tired of saying the same prayers over and over, if I tune out. I get the same question about saying the liturgy at church each week. Don't I crave variety?

I am not sure if it was in saying these prayers each morning or in church week after week, but at some point I realized I was no longer "saying prayers." I was praying them. They began to have a life of their own in me and for me. I looked forward to the words, to the pattern, to knowing there was a set time to confess my sin, to hear I am forgiven. I began to look forward to praying. The set ways to praise God were great because I am lousy at it otherwise. Being reminded that I have been wakened to "praise thee and ask for thy grace" feels like the best possible way to start the day. As Tish Harrison Warren writes, "Patterns of prayer draw us out of ourselves, out of our timebound moment, into the long story of Christ's work in and through his people over time."[11]

If I'm not too tired I say the short Family Evening Prayer by myself, very quietly, at the side of the bed or on it, again with the prayer book in my hands. I look at my pillow longingly. Craig is almost always asleep before I am. It's silent but for the buses, the occasional voices downstairs, and Craig's snores. I'm one of those people who heads up to bed early, but along the way I pop in a load of laundry, fill the dog's water bowl, answer two emails on my phone, write myself a note of things to do in the morning, and answer several texts. Once I'm (finally) in bed I begin, "O LORD, let our prayer be set forth in thy sight as the incense, and the lifting up of our hands as an evening sacrifice."[12]

I'm not an incense enthusiast, but the image of the longings and worries I've accumulated in the day rising up into God's keeping relaxes me. All this weight has somewhere to go, not to be cast aside, but to be held, and not just by anyone, but by God. It's like hanging up my uniform in a locker at the end of the day. I can shed not only the clothes but the responsibilities.

A Prayer of Confession follows this lifting and it's good to be honest one more time. It's a variation on not letting the sun go down on my anger.

> O ALMIGHTY Father, Lord of heaven and earth, We confess that we have sinned against thee in thought, word, and deed. Have mercy upon us, O Lord, have mercy upon us after thy great goodness; According to the multitude of thy mercies do away our offences; Wash us thoroughly from our wickedness, And cleanse us from our sins; For Jesus Christ's sake. Amen.[13]

This prayer's train of verbs—have mercy, do away with our offenses, wash us, cleanse us—unburdens me like emptying my knapsack. I remember God's vast love for me, how He wants to pull us to the freedom I was shown in this morning's prayers. The dust and sweat and weariness dissipate. I name the sins I remember doing that day. I ask forgiveness for the ones I can't remember. I envision their being scrubbed out of sight.

After the Confession comes the Pardon through the Cross. Absolution for our sins is best said to us by a priest, but placed here, far too late in the evening to have a priest in our midst, I'm glad to head off to sleep knowing I'm forgiven.

I whisper:

> ALMIGHTY Father who of thy great love to men didst give thy dearly beloved Son to die for us: Grant that through his Cross our sins may be put away, and remembered no more against us, and that, cleansed by his Blood, and mindful of his sufferings, we may take up our cross daily, and follow him in newness of life,

until we come to his everlasting kingdom; through the same thy Son Jesus Christ our Lord. Amen.[14]

Again these verbs and phrases seem weighted to help them sink in to us: putting away our sins, remembering them no more, cleansed that we may carry on. Redemption is astounding in how personal and how extensive it is.

One of the boons of the collects is that God's work is proclaimed before our request, a sequence that helps me remember that He's initiating, bidding, offering cleansing. He acts first.

The Collect for Freedom from Worry (my sister's favorite) follows the Pardon.

> O LORD, who hast pity for all our weakness: Put away from us worry and every anxious fear, that, having ended the labours of the day as in thy sight, and committing our tasks, ourselves, and all we love into thy keeping, we may, now that night cometh, receive as from thee thy priceless gift of sleep; through Jesus Christ our Lord. Amen.[15]

His pity on all our weaknesses provides yet more comfort, different from the Confession's relief but similarly reassuring us that we don't have to hide.

Near the end there's another gem: "receive as from thee thy priceless gift of sleep." Worries, fears, pain, grief—they make sleep elusive. My friend Ruth knows these sleepless nights well, and on occasion she (like my sister) sends me a 10:00 p.m. text that reads, "and now that night cometh, we may receive as from thee, the priceless gift of sleep." It's become our prayer for each other.

I say the Lord's Prayer and while it's my second time that day, I wish I'd stopped to say it more.

Nearing the conclusion, the prayer book leads me through two Scripture verses particularly suited to its last moments of the day, Psalm 4:8 and Jeremiah 14:9.

We will lay us down in peace and take our rest; for it is thou, Lord, only, that makest us dwell in safety.

Thou, O Lord, art in the midst of us, and we are called by thy name. Leave us not, O Lord our God.

Preserve us, O Lord, waking, and guard us sleeping, that awake we may watch with Christ, and asleep we may rest in peace. Amen.[16]

I rarely pull out my Bible this time of night, but I'm always glad to say, "and asleep we may rest in peace."

Imagining myself relaxing in the sturdy and loving arms of God, Father, Son, and Holy Spirit—I ask Him for the quiet night, and for the perfect end, that at the end of all my days, I may die both in His care, and without turmoil.

THE Lord Almighty grant us a quiet night, and at the last a perfect end; and the blessing of God Almighty, the Father, the Son, and the Holy Ghost, be with us this night, and for evermore. Amen.[17]

Two or three minutes after I started, my mind ready to be done, the buses still roaring in the distance, my evening prayer, like the day behind me, is done.

4

LITURGICAL YEAR

*I*t was a blog reflection, "The Highlights of Ordinary Time," that prompted my deeper interest in the Liturgical Year. I can't recall who sent it or even what it said, but the title was an intriguing oxymoron, and it made me curious. I liked the way the church calendar structured the readings in church so everyone across the globe read them in the same week. I sensed there was something liberating embedded in the way the Liturgical Year reframed time, that it had the ability to open more of the windows to see more of Christ at work in the world. But I was stymied to figure out how.

Then I got mad.

Forging into all the ways the Liturgical Year was laid out within the prayer book—the countless pages of small print with their "Proper Lessons," "Calendars and the Lectionaries," "Table of Movable Feasts," and "Lessons for Holy Days"—I began to wonder if my treasured red book held secrets. I knew I was missing some important navigating skills, but could it be that I wasn't supposed to understand the pages of charts and tables that structured this calendar? That their complexity was intended to exclude those of us who aren't priests?

Wasn't the original intent of the prayer book that everyone could use it to pray, not just in church but on our own?

One Sunday evening, helping to clean up after a service, I spilled my frustration to Harry, our rector and one of my favorite people at church. I'm guessing I threw up my hands wildly and raised my voice with every question. How did all these calendars interrelate? What was the meaning of terms like "Propers," "Trinity," "Red-Letter Holy Days," and "Year B"? How did the church calendar relate to our twelve months of January to December? Why was it so complicated?

Harry went to grab his worn prayer book and calmly showed me enough to assure me that there was no men's club, no exclusion, no secrets. Propers were specific readings for specific Sundays; Red-Letter Holy Days were days of the church year that Christians were urged to focus on events and people in the Bible. He pointed me to a few of his favorites and offered to meet that Tuesday for a fuller explanation.

The Liturgical Year, with its specified readings and distinct seasons—even its colors—has a long and democratic history. Like the prayer book, the Liturgical Year emerged and took shape as a means of helping each of us celebrate and acknowledge God's work in the world through a series of steps, and do so together. The Lectionary, with its charts of weekly and daily Bible readings, was compiled as a guide to reading through all of Scripture in one to three years. The seven seasons of the church year were intended to help us ground the miracle and riches of the incarnation and the resurrection—to live in them. In contrast to the pragmatism and pace of the twelve-month calendar, which dictates what we *do* (and how expeditiously we do it), the church calendar attends to how we *be*: to root us in living in the grace of Christ. Liturgical time pulls our days and doings into God's story. It reminds us that we aren't in control of our lives, and even better, that we live not-in-control together. Advent and Lent are the famous times, but each of the seven seasons of the church year offers ways to grow deeper as followers of Christ. Benedictine Sister Joan Chittister writes,

The liturgical year . . . punctuates our civic year with the mystery of who we are really meant to become. It is far beyond anything civic. It is greater than the culture of any single group. It transcends everybody's nationality. It reminds us of roots deeper than time and stronger than tribe. . . . All the undercurrents of our existence are here: what we believe, who we follow, why we do what we do, and—in the end—where we're going.[1]

Over several Tuesdays, Harry patiently explained the tables of saints' days and holy days and lists of Scripture verses. He showed me that these dates were meticulously listed so that I didn't always need a priest.

Thankfully, my rant forged a bond. Harry valued my persistence and devotion to the prayer book more than he was annoyed at my barrage of questions. As I took on leadership roles at church and saw him more frequently, Harry would tease me, grinning and throwing up his arms, imitating my original frustrations. I'm quite sure one of the reasons the Liturgical Year means so much to me now is because it started as a gift from Harry.

<hr>

The Jewish calendar began with Moses urging the Israelites to remember what God had done for them, to commemorate God's care with an annual meal. Remembering the exodus and the Passover became crucial to their faith and unity. The fourth commandment, to keep the Sabbath, began the weekly pause for remembering. God wanted His people to remember that they belonged to Him and to each other, that despite their moving away from Him, He had not moved from them.

Jesus' life revitalized this pattern, giving the early church a similar but richer foundation. The first- and second-century Christians created an annual calendar to reenact the big story of salvation, incorporating the feasts of the Jewish people as they walked through the events of Scripture in the course of a year—the Annunciation, the birth of Christ, His earthly ministry, the crucifixion and resurrection. The prayer book's tables of daily and Sunday Scripture readings, prayer and praises, feasts and fasts amplify these events and times to us, deepening their meaning and relevance. As poet Malcolm Guite says, the Liturgical Year is an opportunity to "rehearse and re-herald and remember what God has done, what God is doing."[2]

In late November, when Christmas decorations are popping out of every aisle in Costco, Advent invites us to step back, to anticipate in wonder and quiet. I once heard it described as a "much-needed speed bump."[3] In Advent, God *beckons* us. These four weeks shape our preparation for Christmas, telling us we are in a season of waiting in darkness, of strengthening our muscles of waiting, and waiting together. We wait to celebrate both the incarnation, God of all things entering into the world as a helpless baby, and to celebrate the reality of His promised return to restore the earth and His people. At our house we eat dinner most nights in semidarkness, with only Advent candles lighting the table, reminding us that we are waiting in the dark for light to brighten not just the chicken and broccoli on our plates, but the world. We put out nativity creches around the house without the baby Jesus.

In most versions of the prayer book, the Lectionary readings of Advent take us through prophecies in Isaiah highlighting the coming King, the Servant, and the Lord of all. The New Testament reading traverses the epistle to the Romans, where Paul reiterates that "everything that was written in the past was written to teach us, so that through the endurance taught in the Scriptures and the encouragement they provide we might have hope" (Romans 15:4).

The Collect for the second Sunday of Advent echoes this passage,

Blessed Lord, who caused all Holy Scriptures to be written for
our learning: Grant us so to hear them, read, mark, learn, and
inwardly digest them, that by patience and the comfort of your
holy Word we may embrace and ever hold fast the blessed hope
of everlasting life, which you have given us in our Savior Jesus
Christ; who lives and reigns with you and the Holy Spirit, one
God, for ever and ever. Amen.[4]

One chilly Sunday in early December, a beloved elderly woman
in our congregation with wavy gray hair, a gravelly voice, and perfect
posture stood at the lectern of our church and read this collect aloud.
When she finished, she stayed at the lectern for longer than usual
and then looked out at the congregation and gave us all an awkwardly
long stare. I'm guessing she felt we had no clue how true this collect
was, that we must dwell in the Scripture, inwardly digesting its
words, and that it is through that patient intention that we are given
deep and sustaining hope.

She didn't want us thinking hope might come cheap.

On the Sundays of Advent when I stand waiting in line to receive
Holy Communion, I think of Mary, anticipating and waiting for birth,
and the whole world waiting for Christ's return. When we come to
Christmas Eve (the last night of Advent) and stand again in line at
Holy Communion, I am grateful that her baby, who would redeem the
world, was born not in power and triumph but in poverty and ob-
scurity. As the wonderful hymn observes, "how silently, how silently
the wondrous gift is given."[5]

The liturgical season of Christmas begins its twelve days on
December 25, and by now the four candles of our Advent wreath ra-
diate light into our kitchen during the darkest days of the year in the
Northern Hemisphere. In Christmas we celebrate the incarnation,
God *coming* to us, His people. On Christmas morning we give gifts,
not only to bless each other but to mimic God's gift to us in Christ. We

celebrate His coming with friends and family, with a feast—beef tenderloin, scalloped potatoes, and chocolate cake.

At church we acknowledge the feast of Saint Stephen on December 26, one of the first holy days of the Liturgical Year, with related readings and collects. Stephen was the first of many saints killed for their faith, a startling and needed reminder of suffering amid the Christmas meal leftovers and the new toys and books scattered around the house. On December 28, some churches focus on the readings and collects for the Feast of the Holy Innocents, honoring the horror and heartbreak of the babies slaughtered by Herod. These paradoxes remind us of the enduring connection between Christ's birth and His crucifixion, between life and death.

On January 6, Epiphany begins. In these ten weeks we start with remembering the arrival of the wise men, the three kings who were guided by a star on an arduous journey to the Messiah. As the three kings received their revelation of Christ, I think of this as the season when God *explains* the way He will redeem us from our sin, the way He will redeem our world. The first Lectionary reading of this season, the early verses of Isaiah 60, foretells of these events thousands of years before they happened, that God had this all planned. As we move on in these weeks, the Scripture readings and collects take us through the Baptism of Christ, His transfiguration, His life on earth, all so that we might be "strengthened to bear our cross and be changed into His likeness from glory to glory" (collect for the last Sunday of Epiphany).[6]

In my childhood neighborhood, a Catholic family held a "Three Kings" party every January 6 to celebrate their journey and arrival. The street would be filled with cars; their friends of every age arrived with bottles of wine and platters of food and countless children. At the front door the mother stood to welcome them and asked each person—young, old, pregnant, athletic—to remove one of their shoes. All evening we tottered around the house with one shoe on and one off,

carrying our plates and glasses awkwardly, spilling now and then, en-
acting the challenging journey of the kings walking to Bethlehem. At
the end of the evening there was a huge cake covered with fluffy white
icing (my favorite part of the evening) in which a small baby Jesus was
hidden. Together with the kings we, too, searched for Him.

From Epiphany we process to Lent. We have been celebrating
God appearing as a baby (and His ministry as an adult, healing the
sick and making that good wine); now we go with Him moving
toward death. The change feels abrupt. But as the Liturgical Year
intends to offer, just as Christ was hungry and vulnerable to temptation in the wilderness, he also finally had quiet, space to be more
attentive, more openhanded to His Father. As Father Ron Rolheiser
writes, in Lent we can open ourselves to "the chaos of the desert so
we can give the angels a chance to feed us."[7] As we prepare for and
commemorate the crucifixion, I think of Lent as the season as God
giving Himself.

The six-and-a-half weeks of Lent begin with Ash Wednesday, when
we go to the altar at the front of the church for the priest to make the
sign of the cross on our foreheads in ash, saying to each of us,
"Remember that you are dust, and to dust you shall return." To follow
the Liturgical Year is to remember what our culture tries to help us
forget: we are going to die.

Lent offers detachment—detaching from the world's ways so we
can reattach all the more to God's. The collect for the third Sunday in
Lent echoes the words of Saint Augustine.

> Heavenly Father, you made us for yourself, and our hearts are
> restless until they rest in you: Look with compassion upon the
> heartfelt desires of your servants, and purify our disordered af-
> fections, that we may behold our eternal glory in the face of
> Christ Jesus; who lives and reigns with you and the Holy Spirit,
> one God, for ever and ever. Amen.[8]

I need this reminder that my heart *is* restless, and that it's restless because of my "disordered affections" (a phrase first composed by the sixteenth-century monk, Ignatius of Loyola). I give my love and attention to pursuits that do not give me rest or joy. "Disordered affections" always takes me to one of my favorite quotes of C. S. Lewis,

> It would seem that Our Lord finds our desires not too strong, but too weak. We are half-hearted creatures, fooling about with drink and sex and ambition when infinite joy is offered us, like an ignorant child who wants to go on making mud pies in a slum because he cannot imagine what is meant by the offer of a holiday at the sea.[9]

Holy Week, from Palm Sunday to Easter Sunday (the last week of Lent), is a time when we accompany Jesus from the Mount of Olives to Jerusalem, when we walk to the cross. I often feel like I am trudging with Him in solidarity, yet He's walking with me, with each of us all the time. This walking through the week day by day is more unusual for me than for Him.

One holy Wednesday, four days before Easter, Craig and I headed downtown to an Anglican church that celebrates the service of Tenebrae. The sanctuary is eerily dark (you can barely find your way into the pew) except for five groups of seven candles placed around the room. Each time we hear a Scripture reading for each of the last days of Jesus' life, a loud bell gongs—just once—clanging through the sanctuary, and a candle in each group is snuffed out. Death is near. By the end, there is silence and darkness.

On the evening of Maundy Thursday, our church holds a foot-washing ceremony. With low lights and somber music, we head up to the altar for the priests to take off our shoes and socks and wash our feet. A number of years ago we were there with our kids, and it was getting late. I was tired. Jesus must have felt tired too, knowing what was coming, washing more feet as the night wore on. I didn't notice one of our sons, then six years old, slipping out of the pew and walking up to the altar as the line dwindled. He sat solemnly as his feet were washed; I cringed worrying he might trip over the bucket of water. After his feet were dried, he looked over to our family in the side chapel and yelled out across the vast sanctuary with great joy, "Dad! I have clean feet!" He understood the goodness of the servanthood of Jesus better than most of us.

Good Friday is a hard day to sink into, by ourselves and communally. Our church hosts a long service of reflective music and pertinent readings. Isaiah 53:5 reminds us, "He was pierced for our transgressions, he was crushed for our iniquities; the punishment that brought us peace was on him, and by his wounds we are healed." John 19:17-18 states so simply: "Carrying his own cross, he went out to the place of the Skull. . . . There they crucified him, and with him two others." With the service length, people dip in and out of the back, and I remember that it lasts about the same amount of time as it took Jesus to walk to that "place of the Skull."

Isn't sitting and listening for two and a half hours the least I can do?

Like the women in Scripture "watching from a distance" (Mark 15:40), sitting and listening might be *all* I can do. As writer Virginia Stem Owen laments, "On Good Friday, finally, we are all, mourners and mockers alike, reduced to the same impotence. Someone else is doing the terrible work that gives life to the world. Good Friday is the day we can do nothing at all."[10]

On Good Friday, everything, for me and for all of us, depends on Jesus.

As the transition from the season of Epiphany to Lent feels abrupt, so does the change from Lent to Easter. Suddenly there's chocolate everywhere. Really good chocolate. We eat eggs Benedict and the world's finest cinnamon buns for breakfast. Tulips and lilies fill abundant bouquets, proclaiming the reality that Christ has risen, that someday we will celebrate the "eternal feast." This is the season in which we see that God *redeems*—His people, His world. In church we hear verses of Psalm 118 with its amazing prophecy, "The same stone which the builders refused has become the chief cornerstone. This is the Lord's doing, and it is marvelous in our eyes. This is the day that the Lord has made; we will rejoice and be glad in it" (vv. 22-24).

In the fifty days of Easter (marking the forty days Jesus stayed on earth before the Ascension, and ten more until Pentecost) we are meant to keep celebrating, to keep the feast—with music, great meals, games, all to enjoy the extravagant riches of His grace. A church in Southern California gets permission each year to block off the adjacent street for the week after Easter. They bring in food trucks and subsidize them to offer free tacos and dumplings and shawarma for a full week. People eat like kings.

New Testament scholar N. T. Wright insists that Easter Week

ought to be an eight-day festival, with champagne served after Morning Prayer or even before, with lots of alleluias and extra hymns and spectacular anthems. Is it any wonder people find it hard to believe in the resurrection of Jesus if we don't throw our hats in the air? . . . Is it any wonder the world doesn't take much notice if Easter is celebrated as simply as the one-day happy ending tacked on to forty days of fasting and gloom?[11]

I love a great meal or two, but I quickly fade. Without the Liturgical Year, it would be a one-day happy ending for me as well. I have to keep nudging myself to live into joy. I put flowers on the kitchen table for the Easter season; I put that good chocolate in the fruit bowl on our kitchen island. I remind myself often that how I feel is not reality, that we celebrate whether we feel like it or not. I wonder if I should put out baseball caps (San Francisco Giants, of course) for everyone at the table and start a ritual of throwing them high as we begin dinner.

Following Jesus after His resurrection, we focus on His Ascension to heaven, and we celebrate Pentecost (which can be a specific day, a week, or a very short season, depending on the church) when we concentrate on the gift of the Holy Spirit coming to believers. If Easter is God *redeeming* us, Pentecost is God *with* us. It's when we become the body of Christ here on earth, the church. In Pentecost the Lectionary readings and collects show us that Jesus may have gone to be at the right hand of the Father, but we are never alone.

When I came to faith in Christ, I didn't hear much about the Holy Spirit. Was this an oversight, an apprehension that we would be "led by the Spirit" and ignore the Scriptures? Was this Presbyterians wary of Pentecostals? I never have figured it out. But in the prayer book, in its constant reiteration of Scripture, the Holy Spirit is front and center. In all the service liturgies we give glory to the "Father, and to the Son, and to the Holy Spirit." The Spirit, the prayer book emphasizes, is our "advocate and guide," "our consolation," revealer of "the way of eternal life to every race and nation." As we live our days on earth, there is nothing we need more than the presence of the Holy Spirit, to be "with us as we wait." In the Service of Morning Prayer, after we have said the Lord's Prayer and begun the collects, we sing our pleas to God to show His mercy, to grant us His salvation, but we conclude with the all-essential plea, "And take not thy Holy Spirit from us."

Pentecost is followed by "Ordinary Time" (sometimes called Trinity), the season that is probably my favorite. I'm not a person of spiritual highs and lows or notable accomplishments—my life *is* ordinary. Ordinary Time tells us that God *stays* with us. Joan Chittister writes, "Ordinary Time refuses to overwhelm us with distractions, even religious and liturgical distractions, regardless how pious they might seem. Instead, it keeps us rooted in the great driving truths of the faith: Jesus was, is and will come again."[12]

It's hard to commemorate the ordinary, to figure out ways to participate in it that are—well—ordinary. A forester in Scotland, Gordon Brown, writes that Ordinary Time

is the season to fully enjoy the goodness of God. Many struggle
with this idea of Ordinary Time, but it was to redeem this "ordinariness" of life that Christ came and died. . . . It is in the simplicity of this engagement that we are most prepared to hear "the
sound of the Lord God . . . walking in the garden in the cool of
the day" (Gen 3:8).[13]

Some years I have tried to "celebrate" the ordinary by eating locally
in these thirty weeks, forgoing bananas, mangoes, and lemons, which
do not grow anywhere in or near Canada. Instead I try to eat food from
nearby farms and businesses—the earthy potatoes, lush berries and
tomatoes, the plethora of fresh herbs, eggs from local farms. It's time-
consuming shopping and nearly impossible away from home, but the
flavors and personalness bring a fun joy to the table—and the season.

An artist I admire once told me that she uses Ordinary Time to
think more about the saints, reading Sister Clare of Assisi, Irenaeus,
and Ignatius. In reading their books, she's encouraged by how human
they were, how unlikely that they would be listed with a specific day
in our prayer book. "They're so *ordinary*," she told me, "as unlikely
as you and me to do something great. It gave me confidence that God
can do a lot with clumsy souls."

Ordinary Time is long, nearly six months, and by October I find
myself eager for Advent—for a change. I tell myself this is like waiting
for Jesus to return. I get a bit weary and blasé. Ordinary Time
becomes what Eugene Peterson calls "a long obedience in the
same direction."[14]

But come November 1, Ordinary Time nearly finished, we celebrate All Saints' Day. At our church the Lectionary reading for that
morning is Hebrews 11:32–12:2, and it reminds us that "they wan-
dered in deserts and mountains, living in caves and in holes in the
ground. These were all commended for their faith, yet none of them
received what had been promised, since God had planned something

better for us" (Hebrews 11:38-40). All Saints' Day celebrates what God has done *in* the lives of the ordinary and extraordinary, through them, outlasting them. Some churches focus their Sunday service that week on time for parishioners to speak briefly of the saints in their own lives—those who stuck close in times of illness or grief, those who helped financially, the people who showed up to babysit, solve tech problems, deliver warm meals. I find myself wanting to honor the people in the pews around me, some whose names I know and others whose names I don't know, who week after week I hear saying the Confession "with a lowly and contrite heart," reciting the truth in the Creed, praying for the newly baptized—those who keep showing up with me.

The twelve-month calendar is a formidable force. Thanksgiving, tax deadlines, the last day of our summer holidays—their specific dates come to mind far more quickly than the first day of Advent or the end of Lent. But increasingly it's the liturgical seasons that appeal to me more. They carry a joy, a deeper goodness, a colorfulness. In the midst of deadlines and horrid world news, I remind myself I am in Advent and God Himself is calling to me in these dark days of early winter; there is more going on than what I feel. In Easter I try to find ways to seize joy, or as poet Wendell Berry says so brilliantly at the end of one of his poems, "Practice resurrection."[15]

Returning each year to the stories of His beckoning, His coming, His explaining, His giving Himself, His redeeming us, and at last, His staying with us, I remember these events are our story, they're the time we live in, they're God revealing Himself to each of us in the Lord Jesus.

5

PSALMS

*S*itting with Harry that first Tuesday in his church office with its massive wooden desk and the wall of hefty books, surrounded by piles of papers, I was glad for the explanation of the Lectionary and saints' days but surprised by the simplicity of his guidance. "Learn the seasons of the Liturgical Year. Start paying attention to them. Use them as a guide to focus on the life of Christ. Don't worry about following the Lectionary's Sunday and daily readings on your own yet. At home, enjoy the sabbath and go through the Psalms each morning and evening."

Mystified by what the sabbath and daily psalms had to do with the Lectionaries and Liturgical Year, but willing to heed Harry's pastoral expertise, I started to read the Psalms in the prayer book each day. It sounded manageable. Enjoying the sabbath—abandoning laundry, emails, and preparation for work on Monday—felt more challenging.

I knew there were 150 psalms and that they comprised the longest section of the prayer book (nearly two hundred pages in most versions). It wasn't just Harry who thought they were important. I knew the Psalms were poems of complaint, joy, frustration; I knew several from memory because we sang them in church. I could see that by reading the Psalms sequentially, separated into morning and evening readings, every day of every month, the prayer book compilers' intent was that we would dwell in them, be shaped by them together.

Manageable, yes, but appealing? Not really.

As I thought about making a habit of reading the Psalms morning and evening, it felt like another thing to do, another task. I was afraid I'd be bored—or worse, annoyed. Maybe not in the first month, but definitely by the second or third time through. I had led a Bible study on the lament psalms, taken a class on them, read Eugene Peterson's and C. S. Lewis's books about them, heard psalms chanted in cathedrals, and read specific ones by myself countless times. I *liked* them. But repeating the Psalms over and over, every thirty days of every month of the year, daunted me in ways that repeating the liturgy of the prayer book did not.

In retrospect I wonder if my hesitation was because I didn't trust the Psalms. I feared that in their frequency, their emotional outbursts might unsettle my ways of thinking and living in Christ, ways that felt solid and comforting. They might challenge my view of God's benevolence. Surely hearing over and over "Though you have crushed us in the haunt of jackals, and covered us with the shadow of death" (Day 9; Psalm 44:20) would not strengthen it. Worse, the Psalms might ask something new of me—some change I intuitively wanted to bypass.

My resistance was similar to finding out I had to take a thirty-day car ride with someone I sensed I'd find unsettling, or worse.

But instead of disquieting, reading the Psalms daily—twice daily—has surprised me. There haven't been new demands, only new insights, new riches of God's grace. I've heard a range of emotions in the psalmists' voices—impatience, softheartedness, fear, envy, awe, loneliness—that I'd missed. I've seen how the Psalms connect my imagination to their plants, their foods, their mountains, their sea, their celebrations, their resting places. I have felt their personalness, that they are not written as a general voice of the multitudes but rather express their individual fears, discouragement, and hope.

Like the liturgy of the prayer book (so many of its words reiterating the Psalms), the psalmists' poetry has pulled me into feelings that my brain misses. Writer Kathleen Norris observes that in saying the Psalms regularly, "What often happens is that the holiness reasserts itself so that even the familiar psalms suddenly infuse the events of one's life with new meaning."[1] This reassertion happened gradually for me, but Norris was right. The psalms are included in the Scriptures and in the prayer book "to touch and kindle us."[2]

While I had valued the honesty of the Psalms, I began to love their endearing self-centeredness, how frequently they voiced their woes. "For you are the God of my strength; why have you put me far from you? And why do I go about with heaviness, while the enemy oppresses me?" (Day 10; Psalm 43:2).

Simultaneously the Psalms pushed me to become a better listener to God and to be more aware of God listening to us. I often think of Bono's observation that when he was asked, "What's one thing that you've learned about God through your reading of the Psalms?" he answered, "He listens." Then, "What's one thing that you've learned about yourself through your reading of the Psalms?" Bono answered, "I don't listen enough."[3]

The daily reading of the Psalms began to show me *how* to listen, how to hear God in the words of the prayers. On the eighteenth day of each month, Psalm 91 states, "I will lift him up because he has known my Name. He shall call upon me and I will hear him" (vv. 14-15). In these words, months after month, I have begun to hear God's call to *me*, speaking my name, not with a list of instructions or divine insight but drawing me to Himself. I have had moments of hearing the pauses in the Psalms, the way they invite an awed silence similar to when we have heard an astounding piece of music or witnessed gigantic humpbacks frolicking in the sea.

On the first morning of every month I read Psalm 4.

Hear me when I call, O God of my righteousness;
>> you set me free when I was in trouble; have mercy upon me,
>>> and hear my prayer.

O you children of men, how long will you blaspheme
>> my honor,
>> and have such pleasure in vanity, and seek after falsehood?

Know this also, that the LORD has chosen for himself the one
>> that is godly;
>> when I call upon the LORD, he will hear me.

Stand in awe, and sin not;
>> commune with your own heart upon your bed, and be still.

Offer the sacrifice of righteousness,
>> and put your trust in the LORD.

There are many that say, "Who will show us any good?"
>> LORD, lift up the light of your countenance upon us.

You have put gladness in my heart,
>> more than when others' grain and wine and oil increased.

I will lay me down in peace, and take my rest;
>> for you, LORD, only, make me dwell in safety.

This psalm shifts between self-talk—"When I call upon the LORD, he will hear me"—and speaking to Him directly, "LORD, lift up the light of your countenance upon us." Some mornings I think back to my dad's words of wisdom to me in high school, when a boyfriend dumped me, when I lost an important tennis match, when I got a C on a chemistry test. Walking back to my dormitory in the late afternoons (I was at boarding school), I would talk to myself, saying the encouraging things Dad had said so many times. "It's not over yet," "See it over the long haul," and maybe most importantly, "I love you. You're doing great." The lines of Psalm 4 began to be even wiser reminders of self-talk for me in adulthood: "When I call upon the LORD, he will hear me. . . . You have put gladness in my heart, more than when others' grain and wine and oil increased."

I began to notice the psalms' echoes. Old Testament scholars speak of "parallelism," when two lines repeat each other with different but rhythmic words. In Psalm 103:10 the psalmist observes, "He has not dealt with us according to our sins, nor rewarded us according to our wickedness." The second line (and occasionally even a third line) amplifies as well as echoes the first. It was more than a year of reading them before I also saw the echoes between the Psalms themselves—Psalm 1 and 150, Psalm 2 and 149, and the countless places in the New Testament that echo the psalmist's words.

When we read the Psalms together in church—the people on the left side of the sanctuary saying the odd verses, the people on the right saying the even ones—we hear these echoes even more strongly. I love the collective voices around me, the varying inflections and emphases. Some mornings I just listen. But saying the Psalms at home each day by myself evokes a different kind of communal-ness. Seeing the similarity between my anxieties and those of the psalmists of long ago, the similarity between their highs and lows and my own, seeing how frequently they needed to be reminded that their hope was rooted in what God is doing, what God has done, has given me a bond with them, a sense we are all in it together. Similarly, the words of the Psalms connected me to those who are long dead in Christ, to those who had been inclined to self-centeredness in their prayers, to those who needed to practice listening, to those who arrived at the Psalms each morning and evening feeling discouraged and unloved. I began to see how these were "first-person prayers that always kept the community in mind."[4]

Their communal-ness also connected me to the Liturgical Year (maybe Harry did know what he was doing). The writers of the Psalms were living in seasons of planting and harvest but also in God's work of creation, fall, redemption, and restoration. They, too, had been waiting for the redemption—for Christ—and they prophesied His coming. On the days my life feels so overshadowed by ordinary pressures that I can hardly find Him, I feel the balm of being in the presence of those who were confident of His presence for thousands of years before me. When my weeks get too packed and I neglect the Psalms, I am surprised that what I miss is their worldview, their clarity and confidence in God with them in the messes.

Reading the Psalms month after month, I have found I experience them like chapters of a novel. Over the thirty days, I see that they begin with lament, teeter on the fulcrum of Psalm 88 with its despair and darkness, and then move slowly but intentionally toward joy. I see that the prayer book places the depressing psalms of anger (some call these the imprecatory psalms) with psalms that help us see God's good character, His unending mercy. In Psalm 137 (so harsh it is not included in some versions of the prayer book) we find a desire for revenge, but it is read alongside Psalms 136 and 138 (Day 28, evening). These immense feelings of desire for violence are held with the verses of Psalm 138 that reiterate God's respect for the lowly, His protection in danger, His endless love for all He has created. Legal scholar Samuel Bray writes,

> Is the experience of reading Psalm 138 by itself even remotely like the experience of reading it as the culmination, the last Beethovenesque resolution of a tension that has been building dramatically through Psalms 136 and 137? These questions answer themselves. Read the psalms. Read all the psalms.[5]

In college I took an introduction to poetry class. I tried to look enlightened and puzzled at the right moments, but I was a fake. I could feel some of the poems but usually had no clue what they meant. Whatever Blake and Herbert and Whitman and Levertov were saying, I was probably missing it. When I thought about reading the Psalms as poetry, I felt only more hesitant.

But the opposite has happened. The Psalms have drawn me in to their sensibilities and passion through hearing their rhythms and lyricism. By reading them again and again (which I no doubt ought to try with Herbert and others), the Psalms' imagery and rhythms, like so much of the Anglican liturgy, have wheedled their way into my imagination. Sometimes I experience their poetry even if I don't understand the structure or technique. The poetic shifts of tone and metaphors sidestep my search for the literal and the didactic.

The Psalms were written over centuries—probably from 1500 to 900 BC—and from the earliest years of the Jewish people, the Psalms were an essential part of their worship. They were an important part of Jesus' education and worship in the temple. They were a mainstay of the early (and late) monastic communities, the monks singing the Psalms throughout their day and evening and weaving their words into all their worship. By the time Cranmer began compiling the prayer book, the Psalms were an essential component of the Christian life, their presence now evident in every service of the prayer book.

Another surprise as I read these poems through each month—even without feeling the inclination—has been my experience of praising God.

The concept of praising God has often made me feel uneasy. Why does He want that affirmation? Why would He make me for praising Him? Is it similar to sports teams or politicians wanting adoring fans? Does God have a huge ego? It seems so unlikely with a son like Jesus.

The Psalms (and much of the rest of Scripture), as well as so much of the prayer book, call out praises of God countless times. They speak of the importance of doing so. "Doxologies," short verses of praise to God, appear throughout the Bible. Psalm 145, one of the last psalms we read each month, says, "My mouth shall speak the praise of the Lord; and let all flesh give thanks unto his holy Name for ever and ever" (v. 21).

I know I offer praise and adoration at concerts and sports events. When Vancouver hosted the 2010 Olympics, the gold medal for men's ice hockey came down to a tense match between the United States and Canada. Without a moment's hesitation, I joined the thousands chanting "Lu! Lu! Lu!" praising the stupendous performance of the Canadian goalie Roberto Luongo. I yelled myself hoarse and was proud of it.

When I had the privilege of hearing Yo-Yo Ma play the cello one snowy night in Boston, I could have clapped and cheered amid that standing ovation for hours. It was a once-in-a-lifetime performance and everyone there knew it. At moments like these, I praise without hesitation; it's spontaneous.

So why am I stingy with God? I can manage words of praise for God's grace and care and presence, but praise *of* Him?

C. S. Lewis observes that in our worship,

> God communicates His presence to us. And it is praise that completes the enjoyment of what we enjoy. But, for now, we are merely "tuning our instruments." Oftentimes, there is "much duty and little delight" in our praise, as if we are digging channels in a waterless land, but there's coming a time when the water will at last burst forth.[6]

Like Lewis, through the Psalms I have seen a slight shift, that I praise without intending to, experiencing the enjoyment, contentment, even the spontaneity like water trickling out. I believe in my heart that God made us to love Him, to praise Him, but I am still curious why God commands it.

Eugene Peterson felt strongly that it was through praise of God that we worship Him. And worship, he writes,

> Is the strategy by which we interrupt our preoccupation with ourselves and attend to the presence of God. Worship is the time and place that we assign for deliberate attentiveness to

God—not because he's confined to time and space but because our self-importance is so insidiously relentless.[7]

Perhaps my understanding of praise needs to start with abandoning my preoccupations with myself; to start with saying the Psalms and prayer book's doxologies before I understand why.

⚜

Who wrote these honest poems? Many have taught and preached that they were all written by King David, but if lined up with other parts of Scripture—events recounted in the books of Samuel, Chronicles, Daniel, Ezra, Kings, and elsewhere—it seems more likely that King David wrote seventy-three of them. One was likely written by Moses; about the authors of the other seventy-six, scholars are not so sure. I find it easiest to think of "the psalmist"—the voice at that moment in history who was recorded and then cemented into the Jewish oral tradition. Naming the psalmist this way is like naming the different people who lead singing at church. Most of them are godly, thoughtful, artistically skilled people, and our singing is far better for their leadership, but I don't worry too much about remembering their names.

My most recent surprise, and perhaps the biggest one of all, in reading the Psalms daily has been how instructive they are—how theological, how catechetical, how much I can learn from them about God, about the world, about God in and over history. I keep noticing that, individually and as a whole, they show us how our spirituality and our theology interact. As Old Testament scholar Iain Provan says, "The Psalms were sung and said to inculcate doctrine into our souls, . . . to give us fresh perspective."[8] They remind us of our history. On Day 21, reading Psalm 105, we remember Israel's journey, how God "spread out a cloud to be a covering, and fire to give light in the night season" (v. 38) to the Promised Land.

In the Psalms we are never shown that the less we sin, the fewer challenges we will face. Godly people don't have less pain or heartbreak to deal with, instead they have God's wisdom and word to navigate that pain and to cause less pain to others as they do so. They have the community of believers to walk them through it. The Psalms reshape our shallow expectations, showing us life is full of pain and confusion and surprises, but God is with us, His people are with us with love and support if we seek after Him. In all the moments when our hearts scream, "Why did my son get leukemia? My best friend take her life? My mother die in a car accident? Why did I lose my job now?" we can watch the psalmist also facing terrible challenges. Loved ones are stabbed before his eyes (Psalm 10), David is chased down by the king and his enormous army (Psalm 57), people bring false and terrible accusations against him (Psalm 109).

I wonder if proponents of the aberrant teachings of the "health and wealth gospel" have ever read the Psalms.

Early in the morning on the eighth day of last month, sitting with my tea and hoping for five more minutes of quiet in the house, I was reading Psalm 40 and was struck by the first four verses, in which David is in a "horrible pit," "in mire and clay," and God not only brings him out of it (after David waited "patiently," I remind myself) but God *gave* David joy and thankfulness for the awful experiences. David didn't talk himself into feeling that way; he might not even have been looking for a different perspective. God's ways and our experience, our spirituality and biblical theology, can go hand in hand.

His faithfulness to heal our pain through blessing others can change so much (though probably not all) of our own experience. A friend experienced a horrific psychotic event shortly after the near death of her eldest son. When I was with her recently I asked her how she was processing it five years later. She looked at me almost sheepishly and said, "You know, I now wouldn't trade it. God has done so much good in me, but He's also used my experience to encourage others. At the very least I wouldn't want to take God's faithful care of me from *them*."

Reading the Psalms aloud but alone still feels awkward, but like saying Morning Prayers or Family Prayers at home, I know I hear more. I feel more. Like our favorite songs, the Psalms were written to be heard, written for an oral culture that memorized from hearing rather than reading. When we say them aloud regularly, even if we are solitary and quiet, the Psalms scooch into us without asking for admission. Reading Psalm 95 (it's the nineteenth day of the month) and I hear God differently when I say aloud His answer: "When your fathers tested me, and put me to the proof, though they had seen my works. Forty years long was I grieved with this generation and said, 'It is a people that err in their hearts, for they have not known my ways'" (vv. 9-10). I am comforted to hear that even in the scope of His eternity, God knows what it is to find forty years a long time. When I say "grieved," I feel God's sadness more than His anger. It's a strong word.

Hearing the Psalms aloud occasionally makes me think of Todd Beamer, now famous for his heroic efforts to stop the hijackers of the United Airlines jet on 9/11. Beamer asked the air traffic controller with whom he spoke moments before his death to say Psalm 23 aloud with him. He knew he needed not only to say the words, but to hear them.

I still have days of drudgery, but Harry, and the prayer book compilers, were right. The surprises of the daily Psalms frequently bless me, teach me, comfort me. I've come to like my thirty-day car ride companion.

6

BAPTISM

*I*n the fall of 2015, a whale-watching vessel sank off the coast of
Vancouver Island.[1] It was a freak accident, and even now the cause
is unclear. The crew was well trained (and sober); the vessel was well
built and in good condition. Some whale watchers held on to the
sinking ship like a life preserver, while others struggled to swim to
rescue boats as billowing waves crashed over their heads.

Several weeks after the accident, I watched a clip on a friend's
phone that showed a young man frantically trying to swim from the
sinking ship to a small, open-sided fishing boat. He was strong and
agile, muscular fishermen were doing all they could to grab him, yet I
found myself holding my breath as he struggled in the midst of the
waves and frigid waters.

Seeing the rescue, I found myself thinking it was sort of a met-
aphor for Baptism—flinging ourselves into a different boat for
Christ to save us. Our choice is to dare to swim, to get ourselves
to safety; God does the rest. Baptism doesn't include fighting
waves and frostbite, but when we choose this sacrament, we're
staking our lives on a different boat, on God's making our momentous choice—and the life it will mean going forward—possible
by His grace.

Ceremonies of cleansing by water occurred long before Christ and long before the prayer book was composed, but it was Jesus who called us when He said, "Therefore go and make disciples of all nations, baptizing them in the name of the Father and of the Son and of the Holy Spirit" (Matthew 28:19). It was Jesus who changed this cleansing into Baptism, into the means through which we change our allegiance from following ourselves to following Christ, and by which God cleanses us.

The prayer book's liturgy for the sacrament of Baptism embodies this choice so that God can create and confirm new life in us. Its steps and prayers walk us through this choosing and confirming so it might sink deeper into our minds and our spirits.

The service reminds us that Baptism and its life-giving water connect us to the whole of God's redemption—from Noah's Ark, Moses' basket, the parting of the Red Sea, the crossing of the Jordan River, and Jonah's three days in the gigantic fish. Over and over, God has moved us from peril and misery to safety and life. As Paul explained in his letter to the Romans, in your Baptism you die with Christ and through his life-giving water you are raised with Him into a new life.

⸙

If I know a friend or baby is being baptized that Sunday, I try to remember to reread a short explanation of baptism found near the end of the prayer book. I need reminders of what it truly means to be grafted "into the church." The "Thirty-Nine Articles of Religion of 1571" are articulated in seventeen pages (longer or shorter depending on the version of the prayer book), having originally been written as "precisely what this new English church believed once it ceased to take its theological direction from Rome."[2] The Articles, stating the core of Christian belief, thoroughly based on Scripture, were expanded (and occasionally shrunk) several times until they settled into their final form in 1563. They appear in the majority of prayer books across the globe.

Albeit dense in content and style, Article XXVII (27) is a helpful distillation of the sacrament of Baptism. Cranmer and coauthors saw Baptism as a sacrament to be an "instrument" to receive the "promises of the forgiveness of sin" and to be adopted as the sons (and daughters) of God. In Baptism, "Faith is confirmed" and "grace is increased."

<hr />

I had been a Christian nearly four years before anyone mentioned Baptism. Conversion was always the focal point. While I had been attending a Presbyterian church and involved in its youth group, it wasn't until I was working as a cook at a Christian summer camp on Martha's Vineyard that the topic arose. I'd become good friends with two of the leaders, and one afternoon, helping me wash fifty pounds of dusty potatoes, they asked more about my family, my conversion, my Baptism. They assumed I had been baptized as a teenager and seemed to want to know what it meant to me, what was different.

I knew just enough to be sheepish, and I explained that I hadn't been baptized—that my understanding was that my conversion was what mattered, and Baptism was something young parents did largely as a social celebration with their newborns, and that my parents never got around to it, or better yet, didn't want to be hypocrites.

My new friends looked at me a bit stunned, raised their eyebrows, and gave me a strong "you need to do this *now*" stare. They quickly added that I needed to be baptized in the church I worshiped at regularly—not on the stunning beaches of Martha's Vineyard. Their stares spoke loudly.

Four months later, in the midst of the Sunday morning worship service at the large Presbyterian church, alongside two other adults, I answered a few questions about following Jesus and my forehead was sprinkled three times. There was no preparatory class, no prayer book. I saw my Baptism as a public vow of a commitment I'd already made to Christ (a friend described it as being coronated, having already inherited the throne). I don't question my Baptism's validity, but I do remember more about the turquoise dress I wore than the promises I proclaimed.

Unless it happened when you were a baby, if you were baptized in a church that followed the prayer book's service, you probably remember it. Cranmer choreographed a process that ensured you knew what you were doing. Baptism was intended to be far more significant than even marriage and require far more preparation. If you are over twelve years old, Baptism is meant to be preceded by a class (in the early church, this class generally took three years). In my own church, if their young children are being baptized, parents are required to either take the Confirmation class, or if they have already done that, take a refresher class. Baptism co-opts our morning worship service; those being baptized not only walk through the steps of moving into our boat, the congregation reaffirms their own baptismal vows. We make big public promises, we receive grace, and we do these things together as a community because a significant part of what God is doing is moving the newly baptized into a new community, into Christ's body.

On a recent Sunday, the extra cars in the parking lot reminded me that it was a Baptism Sunday. Friends and family had come to support the soon-to-be baptized. Inside, the foyer was packed; there was greeting and hugging and admiring of babies. The chancel (the area in the front for the altar table and the clergy to lead) had been cleared for more people, and on the altar there were large bouquets, a large baptismal font (in our church, a wide shallow silver bowl), and a pile of white linen towels neatly stacked. The front pews were roped off for the families and friends and godparents. The tone in the sanctuary conveyed a happy purposefulness; staff and parishioners were hustling to get organized.

As on all Sundays, our service opened with a welcome and announcements, and then the Call to Worship, to honor His glory and proclaim His goodness to ourselves and to one another. That morning we began with one of my favorite hymns, "O Love That Will Not Let Me Go," and it seemed like such an appropriate start with that wonderful line, "I give thee back the life I owe, that in thine ocean depths its flow, may richer, fuller be."[3]

The priest started with the Exhortation, the proclamation of why we are worshiping and confessing, and today, why we are baptizing. This Exhortation reminded us that Christ commanded Baptism to be "in the name of the Father, and of the Son and of the Holy Spirit" and that we, "being baptized with water, may be filled with the Holy Spirit, born again and received into the church as living members of Christ's body."[4]

There can be variation in the order of the Baptism service. Some congregations place Baptism within the Holy Communion service, some within their Morning Prayer service, some as a service by itself. What is essential are the components, the ingredients. The crucial ones are always the same:

1. the Preparation and Examination

2. the Promises

3. the Blessing of the Water and Prayers

4. the Baptism—the water, and the sign of the cross

5. the Thanks and the Reception of the newly baptized

Like forgetting the sugar in a cake, when even one part gets left out, we miss the distinctives of what we are doing, and the effect is diminished.

For a long time I was mystified as to why the Preparation started with Scripture readings that didn't relate to Baptism. Scripture, yes, but why random readings amid something so intentional? Why were we reading Psalm 66 that morning? Why a passage out of the book of Hebrews? Nowhere in these verses was there a mention of water or even new life.

Eventually I learned that these were the Lectionary readings for that Sunday, that they pulled us into God's Word and the sacralizing of time with the community of believers who are reading these same passages all over the world.

As New Testament scholar N. T. Wright explains, "When we baptize someone, we are participating in the same narrative. We are saying, 'We are on this journey, this is our story and is now your story as well. And if you stick with us, we will help you live out that story with us. That's what Baptism is all about.'"[5]

∽

As the service and the Preparation continued, an eclectic assortment of people in the front pews were invited up to the altar: a young couple elegantly dressed, she in a slim blue skirt and silk blouse, and the father in a trim gray suit, carrying their cherubic baby with a pink scarf around her nearly bald head and enveloped in a flowing white gown; a family of five with two small boys (romping and jumping on the steps as they ascended) and a baby, their mother looking nervous at their exuberance, intimidated by the elegant couple, all while trying not to drop her own baby as she walked up the steps; and last, a serious but nervous-looking young man, clad in black shorts and a crisp, white-collared shirt. Behind them all were five godparents, watching the priest for direction for where to stand. Individually they looked ready for cocktails in the penthouse, a barbecue at the baseball diamond, and a swim at the beach. It cheers me that Baptism, like all worship, is always communal but also always gathers the assorted, that Christ Himself draws the assorted. We aren't a homogeneous club.

In our church, sometimes it's babies being baptized, sometimes it's a teenager, and sometimes it's a sixty-year-old. Family, friends, and parishioners are there to be godparents or sponsors and to cheer them on, to show their commitment for the days and years to come when keeping the vows and choosing a different life gets costly.

⚜

One summer evening early in our marriage, a bunch of us toted frozen casseroles, taco ingredients, and good champagne over to friends who had just had their first baby. We were excited to welcome teeny Declan, and to toast his parents.

The paternal grandparents were sitting on the back deck in resort-y clothes, chatting with several of us. Suddenly the grandmother leaned over, glanced at her husband proudly, and said to me in a low whisper, "He did it. He took that baby into the bathroom and baptized him! You can't wait twelve years! I feel so much better!" She looked at me like her husband had arranged to buy the winning lottery ticket but didn't want anyone else to know.

I was stunned not just by their boldness, but by the fact that the parents, and the people who had loved the parents and child through pregnancy (and would probably be godparents), had been sitting right here while he had turned on the bathroom faucet. Weren't we all supposed to be in on it?

It is easy to wonder about the babies (and children) being baptized. They can hardly make their own choices, much less take vows. I remember a good friend telling me that his forty-year-old son came to him in angst because his seven-year-old son wanted to be baptized. The boy was insisting on it. The adult son said, "What am I going to do? It's great that Milo sees Baptism as important, but how can he really understand it?"

His father, a pastor, replied, "Does anyone understand it? That they died with Christ in Baptism and now are being raised by Him through being washed with water? Can anyone know why Philip was ready to baptize the Ethiopian eunuch about five minutes after he had become a believer?"

While I understand the reservations about baptizing babies and children, I am deeply encouraged by the reminder that we are baptized as helpless people—loved and washed and held before we've done anything. As the prayer book reiterates, Baptism is God's gift to us. Tish Harrison Warren writes,

> Before they cognitively understand the story of Christ, before they can affirm a creed, before they can sit up, use the bathroom, or contribute significantly to the work of the church, grace is spoken over them and they are accepted as part of us. They are counted as God's people before they have anything to show for themselves.[6]

Throughout Scripture, God looks at His people not just individually but as families and communities, as a whole. In Acts 16, after the earthquake in the jail when Paul and Silas go free, the Philippian jailer and his entire family are baptized. The prayer book requires that parents and godparents make commitments to raise children in the faith, and that children wait to participate in the Eucharist until they make their own choice to be confirmed. The prayer book liturgy always assumes that those taking these vows—parents and godparents—are seriously committed to a life of faith in Christ.

As we continue in the Preparation, the priest begins with the Examination—the momentous questions, historically called the Scrutiny, that precede the Baptism. "Do you renounce the devil and all the spiritual forces of wickedness that rebel against God?" "Do you renounce the empty promises and deadly deceits of this world that corrupt and destroy the creatures of God?" They're not questions for the undecided. The parents and godparents are speaking on behalf of the babies and children, and the young man is answering for himself. He looks nervous.

Our priests always ask these gigantic questions slowly. They allow an extra pause, as if to ask, "Are you sure?" We are remembering who we are, messy, hurtful, deceitful, completely unworthy. Occasionally it is just one person being baptized on a Sunday morning, and you hear the rector solemnly ask the questions and then one lone answer echoes through the sanctuary: "I renounce them." I remember the sound of one woman's voice as she answered this aloud. She knew she was committing to something life changing, and others were hearing her do so.

After several challenging questions—commitments to move away from the choices of the world—we pause to pray for the five candidates. The priest prays, "Almighty God deliver you from the powers of darkness and evil and lead you into the light and obedience of the kingdom of his Son Jesus Christ. Amen."

I'm glad for the prayer placed there—amid promises too weighty for my feeble brain to hold—that God is doing the delivering and leading.

We move to more questions, from what we renounce to what we choose instead. Do we really want life through that new boat? For God to work in us, to ask our allegiance in our relationships with others, in what we do and how we do it? The prayer book phrases the question, "Do you turn to Him, joyfully receive the Christian faith, and will you keep his holy will and walk in His ways?" And it offers the wonderful answer, "I will, with God's help."

God's promises undergird everything.

❱❱❲❲

In other Christian traditions and denominations, Baptisms happen on a beach, in a river, in a quiet bathroom at home. The most dramatic one I've heard about was where the new believer flew through the air on a zipline, proclaiming from high above that Christ is Lord of all. The more exotic was when friends traveled to Israel to be dunked in the Jordan River, where they responded to ardent questions in loud Hebrew (which they admitted they loved the sound of but couldn't understand). I've been to several Baptisms early on Easter Sunday with fifty of us wrapped in parkas and blankets witnessing the dunking from the high tide line.

I enjoyed these celebrations, and I've been glad for friends' desire to be baptized, but they resembled birthday parties rather than services of huge commitment and radical choice. As a friend lamented, "It was one minute long—dunk—boom—it's over. It wasn't the beginning of anything." It's nearly impossible to take vows of renunciation and commitment when you fly through the air or get dunked in a fast-flowing river; to know that you are being woven into Christ's body, a community that's been baptizing for more than two thousand years.

~~❧❦❧~~

Following the candidates' and their parents' commitments to turn to Him, the congregation begins the Baptismal Covenant, a series of questions about our own faith. We stand to do this, as witnesses and as participants, remembering our own God-given identity in Christ and the big role we have in this. We aren't here as spectators.

With questions based on the Apostles' Creed, the priest begins, "Do you believe in God the Father? Do you believe in Jesus Christ, the Son of God? Do you believe in God the Holy Spirit?" Some Sundays I'm grumpy and the questions feel long, but recently I was blessed by watching the lawyer in front of me soberly answering the questions, and by the high school student with fabulous dreadlocks answering this last one, "I believe in the Holy Spirit, the holy catholic church, the communion of saints, the forgiveness of sins, the resurrection of the body and the life everlasting," with a huge smile, as if she had the best gift in the room.

In following the Creed, the questions focus on the Trinity—Father, Son, Holy Spirit. Going through them offers a mini-Catechism here and I am glad we answer the questions in unison. I think of it as strengthening our cloth, readying ourselves to weave in the newly baptized, to give them stability as they grow in Christ. We want to make sure there are no moth holes, no threads missing. The Creed not only shapes us, it connects us.

Three more questions (its title "Examination" begins to feel accurate) move our attention to how we will live with the realities that the Creed lays out. "Will we persevere in the apostle's teaching and fellowship, the breaking of the bread and in the prayers?" We respond humbly, truthfully: "I will, with God's help." How else could we do it? These vows convey that we are committing to lives of repentance, of service to Christ, of forgiveness, persistence in worship, studying Scripture—all that we will try to do not just for Jesus, but in the ways of Jesus.

Then we pray a litany, a list of pleas for the candidates. The version of this prayer in the American Prayer Book begins each of the seven prayers with a strong verb—Deliver, Open, Fill, Keep, Teach, Send, Bring. We see the magnitude of God's willingness yet again. Some prayer books condense these prayers and plead for the babies and children that they "may profess their own faith in Christ, that they may continue in the apostles' teaching and the breaking of the bread, that they may resist evil and be quick to repent, that they may run with endurance the race set before them." The priest prays, and the congregation responds with a "We beseech you to hear us, good Lord." Beseech feels apt here, reminding us again of our neediness.

Watching the baptizands, parents, and godparents up front, I see their shifting feet, their awkwardness in being in front of us all, the look in the adults' faces showing their humble hope that they truly can make these commitments, that they can keep these vows. One of the strengths of the prayer book is vivifying the gravity of what we are doing. You know this is vastly different from signing a piece of paper with your fingers crossed behind your back.

❧❧❧

"Godparents" sounds archaic to many, somewhat co-opted by the fictitious fairy godmothers of Cinderella and Shrek, but these adults in our lives can be crucial. Often a close friend of the parents, or an uncle or aunt, these people can provide love and support in ways that parents can't. Kids need their village.

One of my regrets—and sins—is not taking being a godparent more seriously. If someone asked me now, I'd be sad, but I'd decline if I was living more than one hundred miles away. For the ones nearby, I'd be far more consistent initiating a regular cup of hot chocolate, a glass of wine. I'd show up, pray daily for their lives in Christ.

❧❧❧

The Preparation and Promises complete, we focus at last on the water. The priest prays, "Father, sanctify this water by the power of your Holy Spirit."

Scripture shows us again and again that because we are physical beings, God uses what's tangible—water, bread, wine—and saturates each of them with divine grace.

The rector looks first to the couple, and they hand over their beautiful baby to his waiting arms. They look nervous. Is that because she will scream when the water touches her forehead or because they feel they are handing their baby back to God Himself? The other baby and two young boys are next; the younger of the two boys arches his back, tilts his head back as far as he can, as if to expose every inch of his forehead to the holy water. After the priest says, "Nathan, I baptize you in the Name of the Father, and of the Son, and of the Holy Spirit.

Amen," he slowly looks up as if to say, "You sure it's truly done?" The rector hands him a towel, and the little boy very slowly moves his head, as if he doesn't want that towel to absorb even one drop of that holy water. You can feel the congregation trying to stifle their laughter at his earnest joy in the midst of something so solemn.

I feel bad for the young fellow in shorts, standing to the side as the babies and children go first, knowing he still has to speak to the whole congregation about why he wants to be baptized. His god-parents, an athletic-looking couple with blond hair and deep tans, glance at him empathetically.

The rector calls Dylan over to the deep bowl. "Dylan, can you tell us all what has led to your decision to be baptized and what it means to you to follow Christ?" He hands him the microphone. Dylan looks at his feet and then out at the congregation. I try to remember if my kids knew him at one point. It's hard to know how to love and support someone in faith when I don't know who he is. I remind myself I can pray for him and his godparents.

"Two years ago I had an English professor who made us read Coleridge." He shrugs his shoulders. "Near the end of one of the classes someone asked him, 'Why do you like Coleridge so much?' The professor said that as a Christian, he was inspired by the poet's desire to look at stars, at the natural world, and see what it all might be leading us to, the truths that might be revealed by their beauty. I'd never thought about what a Christian was, but I had thought that about the stars. The next week one of my teammates said he had to leave right after practice because he wanted to get to church." Dylan shrugged his shoulders again. "I asked him if I could go sometime. I'd never been. I read *Mere Christianity* and wanted to know more. I reso-nated with being a sinner—not like a murderer or anything—but feeling, well, knowing, that I often did more harm than good. I wanted that freedom that I could see in serving God, and not the world around me." Dylan cringes as if he were odd. "So, I committed my life to

Christ and came to Confirmation class, which was fantastic. Now I want to be baptized. I want to take Communion."

Silence permeates the sanctuary. We are all a bit stunned, and then we can't help ourselves. We clap. The athletic couple looks teary and proud. I notice the elegant woman trying to hold her baby while trying to clap and wipe away her tears. Dylan smiles and looks embarrassed. I wonder if his parents are there, and if so, what they are thinking.

Dylan moves toward the water and dips his head forward. With the priest's three handfuls of water, he is baptized "in the Name of the Father, of the Son, and of the Holy Spirit." Dylan dries the drips and then looks up. The rector then uses his thumb and, marking his forehead, says, "Dylan, receive the sign of the cross, as a token of your new life in Christ, in which you shall not be ashamed to confess the faith of Christ crucified."

After the water and the sign of the cross, we immediately—almost reflexively—express our thanks in prayer, "that by water and the Holy Spirit you have bestowed upon these your servants, Dylan, Sophia, Zachary, Nathan, and Anna, the forgiveness of sin. Receive them as your own children by adoption; make them members of your holy church." This is one of those moments when the 450-year-old liturgy seems spontaneous: it precedes our natural "Thank you!" for these young people and their families, for adopting all of us.

And then more applause. The newly baptized are carried or walk down the center aisle of the sanctuary and then return to the font, shaking all the hands they can reach.

We all walk in faith, greeting one another, following Him, and we do so together. In the prayer book's steps, you prepare, you're examined, you promise, you are cleansed by holy water, you are received.

When I imagine how it was for those rescued from the sinking whale-watching ship, for that agile young man in the YouTube clip, I can only guess how stunned they must have been, but also what a profound experience it was to have survived. As they prepared to swim, to fight the waves, to get themselves to the small boat, to get pulled up onto it, to realize they were going to live, they miraculously were given new life. It reminds me again of Baptism.

7

COMPLINE

*I*t started with the usual Wednesday evening text.

Thinking 6:30 ETA. Does that work? I could bring a salad?

I predictably replied:

6:30 is good. I've got dinner—no need for salad. Cookies?

And then:

Great. See you tomorrow.

They are at our door at 6:28. Dropping their coats on the dining room chairs, we joke about their promptness. There are hugs all around; I'm not sure when the hug ritual started but it's a fixture now.

Craig grabs James and Diana a Coke Zero and a glass of red wine while I get dinner onto our plates. Tonight it is a beef stew, a celery salad, and bread. Diana and James appreciate a good loaf of bread. I like it that they know the difference.

We keep these meals basic—a soup and a baguette or roast chicken and a salad. We rarely have dessert unless she brings her renowned cookies, but James and Diana are fantastic tasters—not critics, but great think-about-the-food eaters—it's fun to experiment on them.

Some weeks my experiments are mediocre—James glances at Diana to see what redemptive feature she will find to compliment. "This chicken is really interesting. Is that some special kind of vinegar?" she'll ask with a warm smile. James grins.

Tonight over dinner we go straight to James's new research. It's fascinating to hear the inside stories. He's working on possible treatments of Alzheimer's and dementia, and the challenges to its success are endless—everything from contamination to funding delays. We interrupt him with questions constantly. Soon we segue to each other's work—Di's a librarian—and that conversation usually moves to aging parents, kids, an injured knee, a car problem, an article in the *New York Times*. Relief settles over us as we let down our reserve, both in what we ask and in what we reveal. It took a year or two of these evenings but there's deep trust now.

James told me once how important our dinners had become for him, not just for the meal but for time to be honest with each other, for how it changes our Compline service. It means that when we get to Compline, we pray it without pretense. We say its liturgy as needy, weary sinners, together. We do so feeling not only known, but connected.

❧❧❧

I was in my midtwenties the first time I went to Compline. Trying to meet new people, I made myself go to the service on a weekend retreat and I thought afterward that the Compline services each night were the highlight. The service leader explained that Compline started in the fourth century as bedtime prayers for monks. Over the years it's been structured differently in various Catholic and Protestant churches, but it's always short, and better yet, it's implicit in Compline that the day is done. When we left that little chapel in the woods, we were urged to skip a late-night conversation or phone call and head straight to bed. As it was in the early monastic communities, the conclusion of Compline was the beginning of the silence intended to last until the first service of the morning.

Quiet and full of God's immanence, the services that weekend were an affirmation of rest: a tiny taste of heaven, when all will be at rest. That night I felt like I was being folded into God's strong, gentle arms to snooze while He took care of everything. The second night I found the service relaxing and restful, as if all had been righted, as if I could see the world in all its messiness, but under it, a foundation of God's calm, enduring omnipotence. Compline imbued this wonderful sensibility that the world, and all that's in it, is God's. Not my endeavor, but God's. The words of the liturgy were far deeper than any the weekend's speaker could offer.

We started Compline with James and Diana eight years ago. James was frustrated with how our church had handled something with a friend of his. Eating drippy tacos together one night, with his eyes darting and his body tense, he railed, "I feel done with church for a while. Not with God, but with church. I need a break from the people."

The day after James's outburst, Diana looked at me with her eyes teary and said, "I get why he's angry. I am too. But giving up on our church?" She threw up her hands. "They're our people!"

Out for an early walk one morning, I remembered how Eugene Peterson often said that when there's great pain, "Let ritual do its work." I wondered if reading Compline together might be a way to support James. What if we shared a simple dinner and said the service together? We wouldn't have a Bible study. We wouldn't even say extemporaneous prayers. James would know he could relax because the service would be predictable.

Eight years later, the four of us have dinner and Compline together nearly every week. We keep our Thursday evenings protected.

Compline was awkward at first—figuring out who would lead the prayers, how to say the Psalms so they didn't sound contrived. I felt like we were saying lines in a play and couldn't get the timing right. Craig said the "leader" lines and we said the responses, but it still seemed weird. James came willingly but I wondered if it was just to be polite.

<hr/>

After dinner and washing up, we settle into our family room chairs. When we started, Craig printed four copies of an online Church of England Compline service, and we have held these copies in our hands ever since. We sit quietly for a minute or two, helping us switch from the laughter of dinner and dishwashing to the quietude of Compline. Craig starts us out: "The Lord Almighty grant us a peaceful night and a perfect end. Amen." We respond with, "Our help is in the Name of the Lord." He answers, "The maker of heaven and earth."[1]

I used to wince that we jumped right into the "perfect end," to the reality of our own death. From the very first sentence, we had to be so heavy? Thankfully, as quickly as the liturgy goes to death, the liturgy moves to our confidence. The sequence and straightforwardness of these statements soften and cheer me—we are naming our greatest vulnerability and fear but immediately nudged to our greatest hope and comfort. I find it a needed reset.

The hero of some of my favorite novels, Brother Cadfael, is a twelfth-century monk. He's wise, funny, kind, and truthful. He muses (usually just as he finds a dead body) about the importance of our awareness of our own end. He knows we live better with our death in view. Late one night, shortly before heading into the monastery's service of Compline, he reflects, "Death is present with us every day of our lives. It behooves us to take note of its nearness, not as a threat but as our common experience on the way to grace."[2]

Our "perfect end" is good to pray for.

After the opening affirmations, we say the Confession together: "Most merciful God, we confess to you, before the whole company of heaven and one another, that we have sinned in thought, word and deed and in what we have failed to do. Forgive us our sins, heal us by your Spirit and raise us to new life in Christ. Amen."[3]

We repent of what we did to hurt others and the people around us—most of which I have tried to forget or ignore. I was exceptionally impatient (okay, rude) with one of my mother's caregivers. I told an editor that I had something completed, but it wasn't. Without Compline I might not have given these sins much attention. Encouraged to confess, I see myself more clearly, and I see more of God's abundant grace. As a friend wrote to me recently, "I've come to like living in the land of cleansing forgiveness more than I like living in the land of hiding."

Occasionally one of us names our sins aloud, but most often in saying the Confession alongside each other, allowing a few moments for silent confession, sensing the tenor of each other's humility, it's enough to know that grace awaits. There is forgiveness not only for each of our own sins, but for the sins of the church, and for the sins of the whole world.

Our confession is followed by a poem, or more likely an ancient hymn. Saddled with a highbrow name for a lullaby, *Te Lucis ante Terminum*, the Latin for "To Thee Before the Close of Day," is most likely a translation of a very old hymn, first placed in the Catholic church's breviary (a prayer book similar to the one used in Protestant worship) and now a part of the Compline service used by the Church of England. I am always glad to hear the words move from tentative to more assertive—from "you would keep," to "by whose breath our souls are raised." I hope I make that transition in my own prayers.

Craig reads the poem to us, but if I am alone I sing it to the tune of the Scottish folk song, "Waly, Waly" (also known as "The Water Is Wide").

Before the ending of the day,
Creator of the world, we pray

That you, with steadfast love, would keep
Your watch around us while we sleep.

From evil dreams defend our sight,
From fears and terrors of the night;
Tread underfoot our deadly foe
That we no sinful thought may know.

O Father, that we ask be done
Through Jesus Christ, your only Son;
And Holy Spirit, by whose breath
Our souls are raised to life from death.[4]

Compline is deepened by its poetry.

After about six months of meeting together I realized we just kept noticing new highlights. One week I was glad for "defend our sight"—something we can't do when we are sleeping. Diana mentioned how comforting she found "around," that God's watch and care are far more present and personal—more multidimensional—than if His watch was only from high in the clouds.

I like that after the lullaby, we move to the Psalms—that we remain in the poetry. The psalmists' forthrightness about their fears for the night and the world to come comforts me. Malcolm Guite writes, "Our imagination apprehends more than our reason comprehends"[5] and I would add, especially when we're tired.

The words of the Psalms often connect our fears with what we know of God's dependability. Psalm 4, Psalm 91, and Psalm 134 (two psalms of protection and one of praise) are the footing for most versions of Compline. The choice of these three signifies that the hour is late. This is not a time to teach new things; it's a time to reaffirm the comfort and solidity that we have in Christ—a comfort I forgot in the busyness of a single day.

Nearly every time I say Psalms 4 and 91 aloud, I notice the psalmist refers to more than twenty challenges—from depression to shaming to disease. Attacks on the sinful and on the innocent are the norm. Reading these psalms aloud reroots us in that reality, and in the promise that God walks through these challenges with us. As I get older I realize I am more afraid of being alone than of sickness or disaster.

Hearing the three psalms week after week (and often in the morning as well) reminds me again that God is the giver not only of His companionship but also His joy: "You have put gladness in my heart, more than when others' grain and wine and oil increased," Psalm 4:7 tells us.

The four of us say the verses aloud sequentially, and we've now done it so often that we laugh at how we wait to hear certain verses, like running into favorite friends. Craig struggles with depression, so he's always glad to hear "You shall not be afraid . . . of the sickness that destroys at noonday" (Psalm 91:5-6); commentators sometimes translate the "noonday demon" as depression or melancholy. Diana loves Psalm 91, verse 14: "Because he has set his love upon me, therefore I will deliver him; I will lift him up, because he has known my Name." She feels it reiterates that we will be lifted and loved, not because we have done anything but simply because we know His name. It is a wonderful distinction.

After eighteen months of praying Compline together, our ritual was no longer awkward but an evening we looked forward to. One night after we'd settled into our spots (we have never changed seats), James laughed and said, "You know, I've told Susan"—a neurologist he works with—"about Compline. And today she said as I was heading out, 'Compline tonight?' and I said, 'Yep. I've got to pick up Di in five.' Susan looked at me wistfully and said, 'I wish I had Compline. You're lucky.'" James isn't sure she has ever even been to church.

I'm lousy at having a full day of sabbath. I'm too beholden to my responsibilities—too afraid that Monday will be too heavy if I don't get ahead of the tasks. Some Sundays are quiet with lunch, a nap, and a novel, but that's only an afternoon of sabbath, of dwelling in the reality that God loves and welcomes my labor, that the world, and all that's in it, is His, that he doesn't need me to help fix it. An hour of Compline is small in contrast to a whole Sunday, but Thursday evenings have become a mini-sabbath.

Two years into our weekly Compline, we made our first addition. After we said Psalm 134 and the Gloria, Craig started reading a chapter of 2 Corinthians. He didn't ask for our agreement, he just started in with, "I thought I would read a chapter." Since then we have read through the Gospels and most of Paul's letters. We don't discuss these passages, we just sit and listen. Some nights we just sit.

We respond to Scripture with the words of Psalm 31:6, the words of Jesus when he was on the cross, "Into Your hands, O Lord, I commend my spirit." It's an apt description of what we are doing in Compline, and we say it three times, like reiterating a promise. Having confessed our sin, and acknowledged our fears and God's great mercy, we are usually more inclined to commend ourselves to Jesus, to trust him with our spirit.

After the Scripture, we recite together "Simeon's Song" from Luke's Gospel (which Anglicans and Catholics call the *Nunc dimittis*—Latin for "Now let us depart"). In the first century, the old man Simeon declared that because he had seen the Savior of the world with his own eyes, he was ready for death. "Now let your servant depart in peace," we quote Simeon. We may not be as old as Simeon, but I, too, long to "go in peace"—to my bed, to the end of my day, and eventually, to the end of my life.

We respond with a second moment of silence. This is also our addition, and I am always relieved when we get to this pause. I need to slow down to commend my spirit, to entrust my heart, my cares, my night, my death to Him. It takes a few minutes.

While we had initially decided there would be no extemporaneous prayer, one night James said, "Let's pray for our kids." Increasingly we do pray, for our kids, our friends, our parents, world events. We name them to each other, and to God.

We close with a collect: "Be present, O merciful God, and protect us through the silent hours of this night, so that we who are wearied by the changes and chances of this fleeting world, may repose upon thy eternal changelessness; through Jesus Christ our Lord. Amen."[6]

Craig told me once that's how he feels most nights: "wearied by the changes and chances."

And then we say the Lord's Prayer together. If I were Brother Cadfael, keeping the monks' Daily Office, this would be the sixth time I'd said the Lord's Prayer today, but for the four of us, at best it's the second.

We conclude with a few more lines from the Psalms, reminding ourselves that "as the night watch looks for the morning, so do we look to you, O Christ." We are people in waiting.

To close, we say together the frequently used benediction from Numbers 6:24-26, "the Aaronic blessing." It is likely one of the oldest poems in the Bible.

> The LORD bless you
>   and keep you;
> the LORD make his face shine on you
>   and be gracious to you;
> the LORD turn his face toward you
>   and give you peace.

As we sleep, as we do nothing, God blesses and watches and gives. Sleep well.

8

The CATECHISM

Late at night, when others are ensconced in a Louise Penny mystery or watching Netflix, I have my light low and my covers high, maybe a small mug of something warm, and I read (rather predictably) about plants. It doesn't get much better than Anna Pavord on tulips, or a new favorite, *The Nature of Oaks*.

I'm constantly mulling over how late I can sow lettuce, how hard I can prune my pale pink climbing rose, why my blueberry leaves are looking shriveled. What is that new lacy white flower in my neighbor's back garden? When I arrive somewhere new, I don't pull up Yelp to find tacos or sushi, I study the trees. I try to figure out why the streets are lined with firs instead of cedars, how low the temperature dips in the winter, how much rain falls in a year. As nerdy as it might be, trees and shrubs are how I first make sense of a place.

But plants—even the most stalwart of pines or roses—can't be understood in isolation. You can plunk them in a pot and they'll grow for a year or two, but you won't enable them to thrive. To make sense of how plants grow, you need to not just learn the Latin naming system but to study the local ecosystem—the soil, rainfall, sunlight, and surrounding plants.

Similarly, Scripture can't be fully understood in discrete parts; you need ways to make sense of it as a whole—the Old Testament, the New Testament, as well as the enduring creeds—to see these as an eco-system, and Catechism provides a way to do so. This enduring system of learning offers a way to make sense of God's ways—what He has been doing, is doing now, and will do in the future. It's the best way I have found to hold His whole story together in your mind and in your life.

Before I'd noticed it in the pages of the prayer book, a friend said he thought Catechism was what "the church needed most." I was mystified; if it was so needed, why was it so rarely mentioned in church, or elsewhere? Why was it buried deep in the prayer book? I assumed what we needed most was Bible study, prayer, attending to the Holy Spirit. It was a long time before I figured out that Catechism offered all of these, even connected them to each other.

To catechize means to teach, to give synthesized information using a question and answer format; it's a system that originated with the Jewish system of learning faith orally. It may seem unusual that a teaching tool of questions and answers is placed in the middle of a collection of prayers, but it's stood well the test of time. Not only does Catechism make sense of the world, it helps us make sense of praying, of the prayer book itself.

⸙⸙⸙

My husband subtitled a book he wrote, "Why It's Tempting to Live As If God Doesn't Exist." By this he meant that in our increasingly secularized culture, where God has been removed from holidays, music, education, and history (and more), Christians have to pay close attention to see God at work in the world, to observe Him holding it together. We have to become attentive, like astronomers on moonlit nights or bird watchers in thick forests.

Yet if we can learn Scripture's history and teaching, if we study the stories of Jesus, the Bible can tell us nearly everything we need to know about making sense of the world, to find Christ in it. As Bible expositor Jen Wilkin writes,

> We read its words and come away with a plain meaning or a personal meaning, but we miss the deeper meaning. We are like a casual visitor to the cathedral, awed by its architectural grandeur but unaware of the symbols the architect has carefully chosen to draw us into worship and remembrance. Our eyes are untrained. We fail to see what we ought to see.[1]

This "deeper meaning" of the Bible is astonishingly well presented (and synthesized) in the Catechism. Depending on the version of the prayer book, the pages of Catechism might be tucked within the services for life's stages—Baptism, Confirmation, Marriage, Burial—or they might be ensconced in the final pages with a list of specific instructions for clergy (someone called Catechism the "prayer book's flyover state"). Depending on the comprehensiveness of the version, sometimes the Catechism is five pages long and sometimes it's seventy-five. Sometimes it's printed in a separate booklet, such as the recent Anglican *To Be a Christian*;[2] sometimes it's in the prayer book itself.

Catechisms are all around us. These tools of educating ourselves to make sense of something, to instruct us, aren't exclusive to Christians. Philosopher James K. A. Smith explains this phenomenon as we are constantly being formed in "longings and desires that orient us toward some version of the good life."[3] Netflix and Disney films form us by vivifying that the surest route to the admiration and adoration we long for is beauty, fame, and money. These films may not articulate questions and answers, but they skillfully catechize us with their plots and characters. My phone catechizes me in the importance of being connected, of not being left out. Studies show our phones implicitly ask us, Might you want to lighten this conversation up because you might get interrupted by a call or text? Do you want to be restrained in your empathy because you might need to go quickly?[4] How do we answer?

❦

Wendell Berry, one of my favorite writers (and farmers), has been described as the catechist of the "lost art of stewardship and community."[5] In his poem "Questionnaire," Berry asks in the initial stanza:

> How much poison are you willing
> to eat for the success of the free
> market and global trade? Please
> name your preferred poisons.[6]

His use of direct questions (each of the poem's five stanzas begins with one) presses his reader to personally consider what they don't know or don't want to acknowledge, and it does so far more effectively than if he had used statements. Similarly (though less confrontational in tone), the Catechism's use of questions shows us what we are missing (or have forgotten). It helps us do the remembering that God calls us back to. By concentrating on the Apostles' Creed, the Ten Commandments, the Lord's Prayer, and the Sacraments, the prayer book's Catechism structures and prioritizes our learning.

Most versions were written in the last 450 years as responses to challenges that confronted the church. Luther wrote one of the first Protestant versions soon after the Reformation in the early 1500s. Redeemer Presbyterian Church in Manhattan created "The New City Catechism"[7] in 2011 in response to the increasing secularism of New York City (and beyond). Baptists, Lutherans, and Presbyterians (and countless others) have created their own versions. Questions such as "How is God like earthly fathers?" "How is God unlike earthly fathers?" "How did God prepare us for redemption?" and "How do we recognize the presence of the Holy Spirit in our lives?" are staples. If taught well, these questions become conversational; they show us where we're missing pillars in the scaffolding of our faith.

⸺⸺⸺

Historically the Christian Catechism was taught to prepare new believers for Baptism, or teenagers for Confirmation, a follow-up process to their infant Baptism. More recently, as so many of us have been raised without much biblical knowledge (and often without Baptism), churches are focusing on offering classes for adults and resources for households as well. Some families talk over one question and answer each evening during dinner, enjoying the combination of the joy of four-year-olds, the skepticism of sixteen-year-olds, and the wisdom of seventy-year-olds. Wrestling through "What is the church?" or "How does sin affect you?" becomes clearer conversing with others; it stays in your mind better as well.

Most frequently, the Catechism is taught as a class within a church community. For several years, a friend and I hosted eight people at our house for a Friday night and Saturday. The first evening we did an overview of the Apostles' Creed, asking questions such as, "How does recognizing God as Creator affect your understanding of His creation?" We discussed where the Bible delves into this, where we see it (or don't) in our work and homes. Enjoying spaghetti and caesar salad, we chatted over why (and if) it matters that Jesus descended to the dead. How does it change our lives if we believe in the resurrection? Saturday, we got a start on the Ten Commandments. "What does it mean to love your neighbor as yourself? What might you covet? What does it mean not to steal?" As we ate sandwiches and munched potato chips, we talked (and laughed) about stealing towels from hotel rooms, how we are more prone to steal from the faceless Marriot than from someone we know.

For several years, Craig taught the Catechism after our Sunday service (doughnuts were a bonus). He moved slowly through the questions, meeting most Sundays for eight or nine months. The group often became a community, collectively making sense of hell, the Ascension, and the virgin birth. A few weekly Bible study groups at our church have opted to go through the Catechism's questions instead of their usual book study. Occasionally a catechist (a trained person appointed by a local bishop to teach Catechism) joins them for six weeks to guide the group through it.

I try to spend a few days revisiting the prayer book's Catechism on my own once or twice every year. I feel the need for the reminder, to be regrounded. Last summer, sitting on the deck in the early morning, overlooking the waters of Trincomali Channel (off the coast of Vancouver), I reread the questions about the Ten Commandments. I noticed that when the Catechism asks, "What is your duty towards your Neighbour?" it answers, "to hurt nobody by word or deed, to be true and just in all my dealings." We have a new neighbor, and he leaves out messy garbage; he parks his huge truck in front of our house instead of his own. Do I consider going over to chat with him about this? Or quietly just cleaning up the papers and bottles? I am neither true nor just "in my dealings."

As I walk through the Creed and Commandments, the questions and their answers show me that I sin against God at least as much as I sin against people, that the ordinariness and hiddenness of my sin keeps me from attending to it, from repenting. The Catechism asks, "How do you rightly live in the fear of God?" and the answer takes me first to the Ten Commandments, then to the Sermon on the Mount. How am I hiding God's goodness, hesitating to voice the ways of Christ? How have I suppressed generosity, or practiced it so that others would admire it?

The Catechism's questions and answers initially seem like a long test with lots of short answers included. Yet the more I focus on them, on my own or with others, the more I notice they create something bigger; they offer a structure far more than the sum of their parts.

Similar to when I say Morning Prayer at home, I try to ask the Catechism's questions and answers aloud—to hold myself accountable for what I've forgotten, for questions I can't answer. Once I corralled a friend to do some questions with me (a nice glass of wine sweetened the endeavor). Her surprise and delight at the answers reminded me what gems these truths are. This past July, after revisiting the Ten Commandments, I spent time reading the questions and answers about heaven: "How are the Church on earth and the Church in heaven joined in worship?" and "What do you know about the unending resurrected life of believers?" Like reading an interview, the questions help me process these tenets more personally. The poet and pastor George Herbert noted that "at sermons and prayers, men may sleep or wander; but when one is asked a question, he must discover what he is."[8] I discovered I didn't know much about heaven.

<hr>

The older prayer books' Catechism often begins by asking, "What is your name? Who gave you this name?" God's interest in me is personal, attentive. After your name (the easy part!), the questions delve into the Apostles' Creed. "What do you learn in these Articles of Faith?" The answer intrigues me for how it's worded: "I learn to have faith in the one true God: in God the Father, who made me and all the world; in God the Son, who redeemed me and all mankind; and in the Holy Spirit, who sanctifies me and all the people of the world."[9]

An early question about the Creed is "What is the relationship between Jesus' humanity and his divinity?" (a challenging one for the dinner table). This takes us to those passages in John's Gospel that show us that all Christ does as a human, he also does as God—the two can be "distinguished but can never be separated."[10] The answer also restates who the Trinity is: "Before He ever became human, he was eternally living and active within the unity of the Trinity." The questions "How do the Father, Son and Spirit work together?" and "How does the vastness of the Trinity meld into the specificity and sanctification of our salvation?" push us further. Theologian Jeremy Begbie frequently explains how it was music that helped him understand the Trinity—that the Father, Son, and Holy Spirit can be understood as three notes of one chord.[11] Hearing them separately enhances how we hear them together, and hearing them together amplifies how we hear them alone.

One of the last questions about the Creed asks, "How is the communion of saints practiced?" The answer always moves me. "By mutual love, care and service, and by worshiping together where the word of the gospel is preached and the Sacraments of the gospel are administered."[12] We work at loving and caring for each other, and a part of that work is worshiping side by side. Through that care, and worship, God holds us communally as well as individually. Psychiatrist Curt Thompson writes that the "brain can do a lot of really hard things for a very long time as long as it doesn't have to do them alone."[13] Armed with love, we can offer care and service, we can proclaim the gospel, and we can receive God's grace in our Baptism and the Eucharist.

❧

Even with my long-standing timidity of poetry, I'm drawn to the poems of Brett Foster. I find myself looking for good quotes in them. They are pointedly honest but never self-absorbed. Several years ago, I happened upon his "Catechism":

> What sort of belief would you say is yours?
> Porous. Calibrated to the times. The week.
> In what ways has superflux affected you?
> Too much esteem. Tuned finely to the body's work.
> What do you fear has not been delivered?

The disease of courage. Will it be required?
No questions, please. Can you see yourself tested?
I have never suffered for anything.
In how many dimensions is your faith?
One thin one, at least. [Aside] Was that a trick question?
What is the single thing that sustains you?
Abiding hope that being here's made good.
Care to clarify? Care to offer last words?
I offer essentially nothing, but enough—[14]

"Calibrated to the times," "One thin one," and the culture's "superflux" (or superabundance) indeed leave me with a "thin" dimension of my faith. Superflux shows up on my laptop effortlessly.

To push back at my own thin dimension, I recently made myself try a small experiment. Every time I felt the urge to check my phone, to ask if it might delight me with a fun text or distraction, I "answered" by quietly reciting the Apostles' Creed. The difference in my reaction, in my mind and in my body, shocked me. At first it was hearing "maker of heaven and earth"; another time it was "resurrection of the dead"; these phrases both calmed and cheered me. After saying the Creed for the fourth time one afternoon, I literally heard myself admit, "*That's* the world I want."

After the Creed, the Catechism's questions and answers concentrate on the Ten Commandments, moving from truth to living out these truths, from the grace articulated in the Creed to ways to respond, to act. The Commandments were originally revealed to Moses on Mount Sinai as a structure for the Israelites to live together, but they're equally relevant for us. When a friend's son was a teenager he saw the Ten Commandments for the first time, and after reading them through a second time, he said, "You know, even without the God parts, people could avoid a boatload of trouble and get along a lot better if they just stuck to these."

Catechism students (or catechumens as they are more formally called) are asked to recite the Ten Commandments aloud and then to answer practical questions.

Question: "How might you use God's Name irreverently?"

Answer: "In false or half-hearted worship, oppression of the poor, and conflicts cloaked with divine cause, people use God's Name without reverence for him and only to further their own goals."[15]

It's interesting that swearing isn't on that list.

When we come to the eighth commandment, we find:

Question: "What things besides property can you steal?"

Answer: "I can steal or defraud others of wages, and honor; credit; answers, and inventions; friendship, hope and goodwill from others."[16]

Despite my friend's son's observation, the Ten Commandments and the full Catechism have a surprising vulnerability. Instead of providing a tool to help us mature in Christ and see God's enduring work in the world, they can be, and have been, co-opted into tools of power for the purposes of others' agendas in a variety of settings. One of the worst examples of this misuse was perpetrated by enslavers in the 1800s, who created and instituted a horrific version of the Catechism's emphasis on the Ten Commandments as a means of manipulating their slaves' behavior for their own gain. Instead of the owners asking "What does it mean to love your neighbor as yourself?" some translated the question into "How must Negroes behave to their masters?" Even worse, they rephrased the answer to this: "to be honest, diligent and faithful in all things, and not to give saucy answers; and even when I am whipped for doing well, to take it patiently and turn to God for my reward."[17] To make this horrific deviation even more awful, some enslavers upheld their use of the Catechism under the guise of teaching slaves to read.

While family dinner table conversations focusing on a Catechism question were not common in our house, one Sunday heading home after church we were discussing the meaning of the sabbath. With the aroma of McDonald's drive-through bounty wafting through the car, one of our sons looked at Craig and asked, "What *don't* you do on Sunday?" Craig thought about it for a second and said he tried not to do the work he does Monday to Friday (and I thought to myself, "and sometimes Saturday"). He said he tried to treat the day as the one in which we live in the reality that everything is done, the reality that God has everything in His hands, that we can take a day off from frenetically trying to do our part. He said, "I can rest because the world is God's project, not my project. It is our day to 'practice' what heaven will be like, to live into that." Over lunch, ketchup packets littering the kitchen table, Craig added that the commandment also calls us to celebrate with God's people, so going to church together, eating lunch as a family (one of the kids raised a french fry in acknowledgment of lunch together), or dinner with friends was a priority.

Some years I've used the Catechism's questions to form my New Year's resolutions or shape a Lenten practice. I invariably somehow center my resolution on my behavior toward my husband and kids; it's where I sin again and again. Am I attentive and kind to my husband when the pressures on me are heavy? Does my honoring my father and mother manifest as grace extended to my own parents for mistakes they might have made? Do I love myself well? Do I give myself time for enough sleep and time alone, mindful that these habits replenish me and are a crucial part of my treating others well?

The Lord's Prayer is the prayer that Jesus taught in his Sermon on the Mount. After you say it aloud, the catechist asks you to ponder, "What do you desire of God in this prayer?" The answer is more comprehensive than I think it will be, and different requests come to mind each time I read it. I want God to do a lot. The Catechism's answer states:

I desire my Lord God our heavenly Father, who is the giver of all goodness,

To send his grace unto me, and to all people:

That we may worship him, and serve him, obey him as we ought to do:

And I pray unto God, that he will send us all things that are needful both for our souls and bodies:

That he will be merciful unto us, and forgive us our sins, and help us to forgive others:

And that it will please him to save and defend us in all dangers both of soul and body; and that he will keep us from all sin and wickedness, and from everlasting death.

And this I trust he will do of his mercy and goodness, through our Lord Jesus Christ. And therefore I say, Amen, So be it.[18]

The order of these requests illustrates a spiritual truth I am quick to distort. My inclination is to worship, serve, and obey *so that* God might be willing to send me his grace. Instead it all begins with Him.

The Catechism finishes with the Sacraments. Some of these questions reflect historical challenges Cranmer was facing in the 1500s, such as "What is the outward visible sign in Baptism?" and "Why was the sacrament of the Lord's Supper ordained?" Some of the more theologically probing include "Why is it appropriate to baptize infants?" and "What is required of those who come to the Lord's Supper?" I have to keep resituating myself within these inward and outward signs. The Eucharist is not solely a matter of kneeling at the altar with a reverent demeanor.

At the end of some versions of the Catechism, we find the encouragement for every Christian to structure for themselves a "Rule of Life," which truly is not a diet nor a regime but a means of helping

us focus on the "essentials" (Cranmer's fine word) of our lives in
Christ. The six parts echo the much longer sixth-century Rule of
Saint Benedict (created for Benedict's monks) and has been sim-
plified for laypeople:

The regularity of his attendance at public worship and especially
at the holy Communion.

The practice of private prayer, Bible-reading, and self-discipline.

Bringing the teaching and example of Christ into his everyday life.

The boldness of his spoken witness to his faith in Christ.

Personal service to the Church and the community.

The offering of money according to his means for the support
of the work of the Church at home and overseas.[19]

The tone of these six relieves me and daunts me. I'm daunted by
the magnitude of what the Rule calls us to do but relieved at its
straightforwardness. Does personal service to my church infer I need
to say yes to *anything* I am asked to do at church? Am I called to be
bold in *all* contexts? I calm down remembering that these callings,
like the Commandments, come as a whole. I am not called to sign up
at every job at church if it means that I will neglect the sabbath.

This Rule of Life, I have slowly come to see, mirrors the broader
prayer book, offering a structure, a trellis to grow onto, a means to find
our lives rooted and ordered and flourishing in Christ.

One Sunday morning after the service, I was chatting briefly with
a young lawyer in a brilliant red dress and shiny gold hoop earrings.
Her glamour and poise intimidated me, but I wanted a cup of tea and
she was in a hurry for coffee. She explained that she was racing to get
to the Catechism class but needed a bit of caffeine. I asked her if she
was enjoying Catechism, and she looked at me a bit surprised. "I only
did it because a friend wanted to; all the learning sounded sort of

medicinal. But it's been fantastic. I have learned so much about my faith, about God. It's offered me a way to see into the Bible so much more clearly. I think we forget that faith is not just about feeling; we need to know enough about God and Christ that we know they are there regardless of what we feel. It's like the prayer book. Catechism takes all these pieces and makes them into a cohesive whole. It feels pretty needed in a city like Vancouver, probably in any big city."

She looked at me and shrugged her slim shoulders. She raised her cup in a slight salute and smiled. "It's probably needed everywhere."

9

HOLY COMMUNION

*I*t was an early summer afternoon. A round loaf of artisan bread was nestled next to a sturdy green bottle of Gallo Cabernet on the grassy slope. As we gathered in a circle, two of my new friends strumming their guitars, I felt sure I was as close to Woodstock and world peace as I would ever get. Overlooking the San Francisco Bay, the sun warmed our shoulders and a breeze rustled through the outstretched oaks. The guy leading our picnic was not much older than I; he read from the Gospel of Luke and laughed joyfully between passing first the loaf and then the plastic cup of wine; he encouraged us to say to the person next to us, "The body of Christ, the blood of Christ." I loved the joy of it all—for a fifteen-year-old bookworm like me, bread and wine and guitars were truly celebratory—but I was totally mystified. How could the sourdough of my hometown *be* Christ? How could Gallo wine, its grapes grown not thirty miles south of us, *be* His blood?

The second time I took Communion I was in the large sanctuary of the church I attended on Sundays. The minister said serious words about the night that Christ was betrayed and how He gave His disciples some bread and some wine, telling them, "This is my body, my blood. Do this in remembrance of me." The somber music felt like a funeral. Tall men in suits walked up the center aisle and down the sides with large round platters of tiny plastic cups of grape juice and small round crackers. Was this the same thing as last summer's Woodstock moment? And if so, why was the tone so dour?

My third experience of Communion occurred by mistake. Early one morning I walked into the back of the church on campus and was overcome by the wafting scent of incense. A man in a long black robe was speaking in Latin and putting crackers onto the tongues of men that I assumed were priests; they were kneeling in front of a wood railing. I slipped out as quietly as I could.

The mysteries were accumulating, and I'm still grappling with them. How can something so varied and so ordinary—crackers and wine—be Christ in us, for us?

Holy Communion—the Eucharist, the Lord's Supper—revisits Jesus' last meal the night before He was crucified. There are accounts in the Gospels of Matthew, Mark, and Luke, and in Paul's first letter to the Corinthians. Jesus was sharing the Passover dinner with his disciples and He added something new. At the end of their meal, He blessed the unleavened bread, which He said was His body, broke the loaf into pieces, and shared some with each of them. Then He took a cup of wine and told them, "This is my blood of the new Covenant, which is shed . . . for many," and He shared that with each of them too. Luke and Paul tell us that Jesus instructed the disciples to repeat the sharing of bread and wine, of His body and blood, as often as they gathered together.

How could ordinary bread and wine become Christ's body and blood for us? Why did Jesus choose a simple meal to do all this? Why not a five-course meal served at sunrise on a mountaintop? Priest and writer Henri Nouwen writes,

> The Eucharist is the most ordinary and the most divine gesture imaginable. That is the truth of Jesus. So human, yet so divine; so familiar, yet so mysterious; so close, yet so revealing! But that

is the story of Jesus. . . . It is the story of God who wants to come close to us, so close that we can see him with our own eyes, hear him with our own ears, touch him with our own hands; so close that there is nothing between us and him, nothing that separates, nothing that divides, nothing that creates distance.[1]

What I slowly learned was that Holy Communion embodies the story that holds our lives, God's continuous love for His people, the same story that places us within creation, rebellion, redemption, and restoration. To learn this story so well that it becomes our daily reality, it's a huge help to act it out.

Communion is mysteriously but tangibly a meal in which we celebrate the past, remembering God's acts of salvation for His people and the saints that have been at this table for two thousand years before us. It's a meal we celebrate now, reenacting Christ's meal with the disciples, taking in His body and blood that He shed for us. And it's a meal we are celebrating the future; it's our foretaste of heaven, of unending meals with Christ Himself.

My early visits to Anglican services of Holy Communion only brought more questions. The Communion service seemed like countless steps—sitting, kneeling, standing—while we confessed, praised, and listened to Scripture. Why did everything we read aloud start with "We"—"We are humbly sorry," "We do not presume"? How could we say all these things together if we hadn't agreed beforehand? What was the relationship of other parts of the service—the Offering, the Creed—to this Communion? Why were these steps in the service always together?

Like Morning Prayer, the service of Holy Communion begins with the Opening Sentence—a line or two of Scripture that the priest reads to pull us in, to reorient us to God's Word as our starting point. It also begins with the same steppingstones, taking us through the pattern of sin-grace-faith.

Together, we say the Collect for Purity: "Almighty God, unto whom all hearts be open, it all desires known, and from whom no secrets are hid: Cleanse the thoughts of our hearts by the inspiration of thy Holy Spirit, that we may perfectly love thee, and worthily magnify thy holy Name; through Christ our Lord. Amen."[2]

My shoulders relax when we come to the words "no secrets are hid." My racing mind says a "phew." I don't have to try to appear holier than I am. We are called to worship without pretense. I used to think of this opening collect as an early confession, that we were admitting we need to be cleansed in order to love God—but now I know it's a plea, a plea that God Himself will prepare each of us to love Him, that God will enable us to do what we can't do ourselves.

A friend says that the Collect for Purity makes her think of Japanese restaurants in small villages where the owners personally wash your feet before you enter the house; a purification to welcome you, not to avoid cleaning the floor.

But how can I do anything "perfectly," much less "worthily"? How can anyone? One morning in church our rector paused the service for a moment and explained that "worthily" did not mean to be proficient, but to "be in humility."

This collect is followed by the reading of the Ten Commandments (or at least several of them), the law. Like searchlights over a dark field, the Commandments reveal how badly we need God's grace, His cleansing towel. While I didn't murder or steal towels this past week, I did not love my family as myself, nor my friends. I doubt I loved God with all my heart and soul for even one minute.

There is an acerbic moment in Flannery O'Connor's story "Revelation" when the main character, the very proper Mrs. Turpin, is trying to make sense of her sin. She's a well-heeled, successful pig farmer in the Deep South in the 1940s—a generous, upright woman by her own estimation—but others are conveying to her that she's not as good as she assumes. On a grim autumn afternoon near sunset, standing in the middle of one of her vast fields, she hisses at God: "'What do You send me a message like that for?' she said in a low fierce voice, barely above a whisper but with the force of a shout in its concentrated fury. 'How am I a hog and me both? How am I saved and from hell too?'"[3]

Mrs. Turpin and I are alike.

The Commandments are usually followed by the Kyrie and Gloria, joyful moments we stand to invoke the Trinity—"Christ have mercy, Lord Have mercy"—and to praise God for calling His people to meet Him in worship. Church historian Lauren Winner wrote that as we stand singing the Gloria, when we sing "Glory to God in the highest, and peace to his people on earth," she is reminded of the shepherds in Bethlehem two thousand years ago, who heard those words and became aware that perhaps more was going on in a nearby stable than was apparent.[4]

We sit for the Scripture readings and the sermon, for a range of ways to remember who God is, what He has done for His people. I'm glad for their wisdom, and their variety.

Like a good cleanup batter, the Nicene Creed follows the sermon, awaiting with its sturdy, substantive framework. It draws me homeward. While we say the Apostles' Creed at Morning and Evening Prayer and Baptism, in Holy Communion we say the Nicene Creed, and we say it in the plural. "We believe in one God, We believe in one Lord, Jesus Christ, We believe in the Holy Spirit." The Creed and our shared commitment not only root and unify us, but they also move us outward, to all that is "visible and invisible," "through whom all things were made."

We respond to the Creed by kneeling for prayers, prayers for our world, so desolate in so many places, and prayers for each other. The duality of the global and the personalness of our prayers mimic the Creed. Christ is for all of us, Christ is for each of us.

I sense a subtle change in the tone of our service after we get up off our knees. Perhaps we have taken off our jackets of outward appearances and settled into being struggling souls together; having acknowledged that we arrived empty-handed, needing to praise God even if it doesn't feel spontaneous, committing to the countercultural words of the Creed, we relax. We know we're all hungry for the riches of His grace.

The rector says the Call to Confession:

> YE that do truly and earnestly repent you of your sins, and are in love and charity with your neighbours, and intend to lead the new life, following the commandments of God, and walking from henceforth in his holy ways: Draw near with faith, and take this Holy Sacrament to your comfort: and make your humble confession to Almighty God, meekly kneeling upon your knees.[5]

Sometimes I have a "Do I?" moment here. "Truly and earnestly"? Many Sundays I am not so earnest in my repentance, I'm only earnest to be earnest. I once asked a priest about the absence of integrity in my earnestly wanting to repent, and he looked at me with incredulity, and said, "Are any of us? Ever?"

Other Sundays, while earnest may be exaggeration, I am eager for Confession. I know I was stingy with my money, dismissive to someone I don't like, spoke unkindly about a colleague rather than going to speak to them directly. I've come wanting forgiveness.

The Call to Confession makes me ask myself, "Is there anyone I refuse to forgive?" Is it right to receive God's gift if I'm not, as the prayer book names, "in love and charity with [my] neighbor?" When Craig and I have an argument, I'd rather stay mad, nurse my grudge. I don't want to be in love and charity with my husband. I want to hurt him back. On those days I stay sitting in the pew.

The Prayer of Confession is also unique to the Holy Communion service. We kneel to say:

Almighty God, Father of our Lord Jesus Christ, Maker of all things, Judge of all men: We acknowledge and confess our manifold sins and wickedness, Which we from time to time most grievously have committed, By thought, word, and deed, Against thy Divine Majesty. We do earnestly repent, And are heartily sorry for these our misdoings. Have mercy upon us, most merciful Father; For thy Son our Lord Jesus Christ's sake, Forgive us all that is past; And grant that we may ever hereafter Serve and please thee In newness of life, To the honour and glory of thy Name; Through Jesus Christ our Lord. Amen.[6]

We repent for what we have done and left undone, returning us to the core of the Ten Commandments—that we have not loved God with our whole heart, and not loved our neighbor as ourselves. It's these commands we keep returning to—for in breaking them, we wound our families and our friends, we fling out our prejudices, we let loose our angry selves.

As in Morning Prayer, Confession is followed by the Absolution, that we might have mercy, pardon, deliverance, confirmation, and strength. There is no discussion between Mom and Dad to decide on your punishment, no pause while God contemplates your worthiness. We are forgiven immediately.

There is a magnificent absurdity about God's forgiveness. We will sin again soon, hurt or judge or ignore, maybe even before we leave the sanctuary. There is no other dynamic like this in our lives—a vast generosity that arrives knowing it will be forsaken, and never leaves.

We move from the Absolution to the Comfortable Words, Scripture verses included for our mutual "strengthening, encouraging."[7] Several Sundays ago the priest chose the words of 1 John 2:1-2, "If anybody does sin, we have an advocate with the Father—Jesus Christ, the Righteous One. He is the atoning sacrifice for our sins, and not only for ours but also for the sins of the whole world." In Christ is the redemption of the sins of *the whole world*—in my kitchen, in the greed of nations, in the damage that we cause in the waters of the ocean.

Having been absolved and comforted, we pause to Pass the Peace, to greet those around us by offering the peace of Christ to each other, "to be with your spirit." There's a happy chatter in the sanctuary again; we are mostly glad to greet one another Sunday after Sunday, glad to meet new people. The "we" in the Creed becomes more genuine.

The service steps forward again, as we give our offering and sing a hymn as we pass the silver bowls. The Offering is our way of giving back to God. I get nostalgic thinking that even seventy-five years ago, we might not have put lifeless dollar bills (or made an e-transfer) in a bowl but brought fresh eggs or bushels of wheat; we would have placed a personal extension of our daily lives on the steps up to the altar and had the pleasure of seeing what others brought.

We continue with the Sursum Corda, which means "Lift up your hearts" and the Sanctus, the hymn of "Holy, Holy, Holy, Heaven and earth are full of your glory," musical praise to prepare us to celebrate the receiving of Christ into ourselves.

Next we kneel, and the priest retells the account of Jesus giving the Last Supper to His disciples. This Prayer of Consecration takes us back to that heartbreaking night in Jerusalem, not much more than twelve hours before Jesus was nailed to the cross. Placing his hand on the loaf of bread, the rector repeats Christ's words. "Take, eat. This is my Body, which is given for you: Do this in remembrance of me." Lifting the chalice of wine, which represents all the wine we will consume, he says, "Drink this, all of you; for this is my Blood of the New Covenant, which is shed for you, and for many, for the forgiveness of sins: . . . do this in remembrance of me." Holding up the chalice, he holds up all of history and God's faithfulness. As Nouwen said, a gesture "so ordinary and so divine."[8]

Still on our knees, we acknowledge that we are entirely unworthy to receive this. We pray the Prayer of Humble Access—among my favorites of all of Cranmer's prayers. We come "trusting . . . in your abundant and great mercies" because, as the service has helped us to see—if we haven't realized it already—"we are not worthy so much as to gather up the crumbs under your table." Together we say,

> We do not presume to come to this your table, O merciful Lord, trusting in our own righteousness, but in your abundant and great mercies. We are not worthy so much as to gather up the crumbs under your table; but you are the same Lord, whose character is always to have mercy. Grant us, therefore, gracious Lord, so to eat the flesh of your dear Son Jesus Christ, and to drink his blood, that our sinful bodies may be made clean by his body, and our souls washed through his most precious blood, and that we may evermore dwell in him, and he in us. Amen.[9]

In our prayer we hear Mark 7:28, where the young woman says to Jesus, "Lord, even the dogs under the table eat the children's crumbs," and Luke 7:6, when the highly regarded centurion said to Jesus, "Lord, don't trouble yourself, for I do not deserve to have you come under my roof," and then Paul in his first letter to the Corinthians, "Is not the cup of thanksgiving for which we give thanks a participation in the blood of Christ? And is not the bread that we break a participation in the body of Christ?" (1 Corinthians 10:16).

We continue our prayer singing, asking the Lamb of God to take "away the sin of the world. Grant us your peace." Singing seems to carry our plea to God with an added dimension, enables it to come from a deeper place in us.

Quiet music begins as the Communion Servers go forward to the altar. We watch each of them receive the bread and then the wine, and while these six people are young, old, Asian, Latin American, and Caucasian, in a gray wool suit, in fraying jeans, their humble stance and bowed heads show us that serving this bread and wine is something we can do only because Christ has given Himself so selflessly to us. No one is worthy to serve or to receive. We are hungry people gathered around our wooden table and across the world. A friend once visited a church in San Jose, and in their Communion service, they offered not just a loaf of bread, but Pita, Chapatti, Naan, Injera, Tortillas, and European rye. The Eucharist is an international meal. Worship is crosscultural hospitality.

Those in the front pews move to the center aisle to line up to go forward to receive. We line up similarly to how we pay for our groceries or board a plane, but this is different. Our line is a snapshot of who we are: needy, undeserving souls, waiting for help, for love in a meal.

We stand or kneel with our hands together and held flat. "The body of Christ, given for you, Julie." As the rector places the morsel of bread on my palm and I eat it, tasting its wheat and yeast, I can see the big cross above me. I see Christ with His outstretched arms, dying for love. It's more than I can hold.

These small pieces of bread often make me think of the British hostage negotiator Terry Waite. Imprisoned in solitary confinement in Lebanon for five years, each morning he would save a bit of bread and water from his breakfast and say the Communion service to himself. In his imagination he was taking part in this act with others around the world. I imagine that I am taking it with those in prison, with Terry Waite, now back in his village parish in rural England.[10]

The wine in our church is currently parceled out in little cups (pre-Covid-19 it was offered in a chalice and hopefully will be again), and we hold it with our fingers while the server says, "The blood of Christ shed for you; drink this in remembrance that Christ's blood was shed for you and be thankful." I can hear him say to our good friends who move through the line ahead of us: "Ruth, the body of Christ, shed for you; Rod, the blood of our Lord Jesus Christ, preserve your body and soul to everlasting life." I'm grateful for Christ's death for those I love.

We return to our pew, as writer Nora Gallagher says, "to let communion seep in, so when my brain decided it was unimportant, I have a cellular memory."[11] We watch others wait in line, watch them receive these gifts.

When everyone has been forward, we kneel again, this time to say the Lord's Prayer together and to express our thanks for the meal, and for all it brings.

> Heavenly Father, we thank you for feeding us with the spiritual food of the most precious Body and Blood, of your Son our Savior Jesus Christ; and for assuring us in these holy mysteries, that we are living members of the body of your Son, and heirs of your eternal kingdom. And now, Father, send us out to do the work you have given us to do, to love and serve you as faithful witnesses of Christ our Lord. To him, to you, and to the Holy Spirit, be honor and glory, now and for ever. Amen.[12]

At the end of this, we sing. I feel like this is when we should sing Charles Wesley's eighteenth-century hymn, "And Can It Be?" with its words, "Tis mercy all, immense and free; For, O my God, it found out me," but frequently we sing something contemporary, "In Christ Alone," or "How Deep the Father's Love for Us."

The service concluded, one of the priests calls out from the back to the sanctuary, "Let us go forth in the name of Christ."

And we reply, with renewed gladness, "Thanks be to God."

Since my days on the sunny hillside and the big platters of the little cups, I have come to wonder if Communion was not a regular part of those communities of faith because to hold the service in all its fullness, including Confession, felt too raw, too countercultural to do regularly. Admitting what a mess we are and have made of the world does not feel like part of the "good news." It's a downer to our welcoming, to throwing open our doors. But like Easter, when we need to be throwing our caps high in the air with a communal "Yes!" and like the Creed that tells us who we are so we can live into the great story rather than having to make up our own story, Holy Communion is the best of meals, a foretaste of the finest of feasts offered in love. It's the humble ordinary, changing everything.

10

In SICKNESS
and in DEATH

*I*first felt death's hovering when I was in labor with our oldest child. I was thirty-four weeks along, and countless possible problems were arising. By the time the doctors decided the birth was unstoppable and I was wheeled into the delivery room, what felt like whole teams of specialists were waiting in the wings, staring at me as if I were a specimen. After several hours of contractions, our wonderful (and laconic) obstetrician abruptly announced, "I want that baby out of there. Now."

Five minutes and two forceps later, Andrew was in the world, teeny and blue and alive.

At nine o'clock that night, our rector Harry appeared at the door of my hospital room. He skipped even an initial chat, raised his eyebrows, and nodded, acknowledging the terrifying day. Deep-voiced and shy, he muttered, "How are you?" and then lowered his six-foot, six-inch frame to his knees. Harry handed me a prayer book, opened his own, put his elbows on my bed, bowed his head, and was silent. Then he began reading the prayer book's "Thanksgiving for the Birth of a Child."

My guess was that knowing the shock and trauma of the day, he thought this service would calm and bless me more than a chat.

Harry, again, was right. That service gave Andrew's precarious arrival a landing. The short bedside service felt like a close friend's comfort. It was one of the early times I felt as if the prayer book was *for* me.

The liturgy began with expressions of gratitude, first in a prayer, and then in the words of Psalm 116:8, "You have delivered my soul from death, my eyes from tears, and my feet from stumbling." That was how I felt in that delivery room. Andrew wobbled near death; if he had died, a bit of my soul would have died with him and my feet would have slipped into despair. God, in His mercy, saved Andrew, and saved me. His mercy doesn't always show up this way, but I was grateful that day it had.

Harry and I read responsively:

O Lord, save this woman thy servant;
Who putteth her trust in thee.
Be thou to her a strong tower;
From the face of her enemy.
Lord, hear our prayer;
And let our cry come unto thee.[1]

Together we said the Lord's Prayer. At the end, I thought, this was not just a rector and a new mother beseeching God for His care, this was a conversation. In the alternating of prayer and Scripture, the back and forth, back and forth, I realized we were not just saying words to God, we were talking together.

At the end Harry prayed,

O GOD, whose ways are hidden and thy works most wonderful, who makest nothing in vain and lovest all that thou hast made: Comfort thou thy servants, whose hearts are sore smitten and oppressed; and grant that they may so love and serve thee in this

life, that they may obtain the fulness of thy promises in the world
to come; through our Lord Jesus Christ. Amen.[2]

"Sore smitten," as Brontë-ish as it sounded, was exactly how my
heart felt. Yet what I thought about for months after my delivery, and
my subsequent deliveries, was the phrase "God, whose ways are
hidden and thy works most wonderful."

⁕⚜⚜⚜⁕

Over the next few years, raising children and losing parents and good
friends through sickness and death, I saw the multitude of such descriptions and phrases in the prayer book for moments such as this.
Ministrations for the Sick, Ministrations for the Dying, and the Order
for the Burial of the Dead were all there waiting, available to replace
the chatting and awkward silences with well-chosen words of vali-
dation, comfort, and hope.

Death came close again five years later. One of my husband's
graduate students had so many hard things happen to her every week
that I found myself hesitating to ask, "How are you?" Miriam came
from a family that supported simplistic hope and answers—promises
of God's triumph and healing if only we have enough faith. It sounded
like so much work: if she conjured up enough faith, she could move
mountains. Amid job problems, family dysfunction, and financial
struggles, not to mention academic demands, Miriam's challenges
were enormous. Thankfully, her four-year-old daughter was a bright
spot, a harbinger of hope. Miriam was soon pregnant with a second
child, and she and her husband were thrilled.

But when she was thirteen weeks along, Miriam found out she
was having twins—and almost immediately, her doctor started expressing concern. We'd have tea together and she'd unpack the new
bad news. Heart problems, lung problems. I admired Miriam and I
ached for her. The babies—whom they named Grace and Mary—
kept growing, and Miriam took care of her body with precision. She

cheered those babies on without ceasing. We all did. We prayed
for healing.

Within a few months, the medical specialists pressured her to induce
a preterm delivery, but Miriam refused. One afternoon she called me at
home. The twins had spontaneously been born the night before. Grace
had died in delivery. Would I come over and pray with them before
Mary died? They thought she might have twenty-four hours.

As I grabbed my jacket, Craig called out, "Take your prayer book.
It might have something." Were there prayers for such moments as this
in there?

I drove over in a hurry, begging God to give me good words,
prayers to comfort and sustain. And as I sat in my car, gearing up to
go inside, there they were: Prayers for the Death of a Child. Could
they have been waiting for 450 years to help me?

I walked into their cozy apartment and Mary was bundled tight
in a soft pink blanket, surrounded by her mother's arms. Miriam's
husband sat in the armchair across from them, his face covered in tears.
It was heart-wrenching. They were exhausted with loving their
daughters with all their might, trying to help a three-pound baby live,
and die, well.

Why was I there and not one of our church's clergy? Inadequate
(and panicked) fails to describe how I felt.

I rubbed my fingers over Mary's matchstick arms and squeezed
Miriam's arm affectionately. "How are you?" was hardly appropriate.
I sat down and looked at them both. There was a long, awkward si-
lence. All I could manage to say was, "Can I pray?"

I started with the collect I'd found in the car.

Lord Jesus Christ, Good Shepherd of the sheep, you gather your
lambs in your arms and carry them in your bosom: We commend
to your loving care, Mary. Relieve her pain, guard her from all
danger, restore to her your gifts of gladness and strength, and

raise her up to a life of service to you. Hear us, we pray, for your dear Name's sake. Amen.[3]

We sat longer in that silence. Mary making tiny gurgling noises, tears streaming down all our cheeks, me hoping for a few more words that might fit the moment. At last Miriam said, "It means so much to me that we could pray for her gladness"—she sniffled and smiled—"and that I can know she is gathered into Jesus' arms—that Jesus will carry Mary and Grace—and that she can be raised up to be of service. That Mary and Grace aren't done."

We sat in more silence, and I read the prayer book's Scripture for the death of a child from Matthew 18.

> At the same time came the disciples unto Jesus, saying, Who is the greatest in the kingdom of heaven? And Jesus called a little child unto him, and set him in the midst of them, and said, Verily I say unto you, Except ye be converted, and become as little children, ye shall not enter into the kingdom of heaven. Whosoever therefore shall humble himself as this little child, the same is greatest in the kingdom of heaven. And whoso shall receive one such little child in my name, receiveth me. Take heed that ye despise not one of these little ones; for I say unto you, that in heaven their angels do always behold the face of my Father which is in heaven.[4]

And then I read another of the collects for such a time as this (to my surprise, the same collect that Harry had read to me in the hospital):

> O GOD, whose ways are hidden and thy works most wonderful, who makest nothing in vain and lovest all that thou hast made: Comfort thou thy servants, whose hearts are sore smitten and oppressed; and grant that they may so love and serve thee in this life, that together with this thy child, they may in the world to come obtain the fullness of thy promises; through our Lord Jesus Christ. Amen.[5]

Until that afternoon, I had never known there were specific prayers in the prayer book for when the person dying is a child. I had never heard prayers that articulated the deep injustice we feel when babies and children die. I had assumed the prayer book would have focused on comfort, on God's eternal goodness (and it certainly offers both in abundance), but here Cranmer selected a prayer that delved into the heartbreak rooted in the world going terribly wrong. His first wife had died in childbirth. He knew pain.

Mary died that evening, nestled in her mother's arms.

A week later their church community hosted a funeral at their small church. More than a hundred people crowded in, including a woman who was one of the finest flautists in Canada and who had lost her own baby at twenty-five weeks years earlier. She chose to honor Grace and Mary with one of the most stirring musical moments I've ever heard. A few of the same prayers and collects were said, this time in unity. I heard them like an echo, God's reminder that He was with us, that the truth held.

The prayer book's ministrations (or provisions of care) to the sick and to the dying are full of sensitive flexibility. They include a number of italicized notes, suggesting where the clergy can include Confession and/or Communion, or skip them both. There is a provisional service for The Laying On of Hands and Anointing with Oil. The minister has discretion to do what is suitable, and if she or he can't be present, then a layperson can preside. It's one of the more flexible sections of the entire liturgy, and again, we see Cranmer's concerted compassion to the sick and dying, to the heartbroken.

These liturgical options begin with choices of Scripture readings, selections of passages in the Bible that express how hard these experiences are to endure. The readings name what God has done ahead of this moment, the ways He has prepared to comfort and carry us, and—equally important—the way God gives value and redemption to our suffering, without bypassing its pain or its longevity.

In the prayer book, comfort, empathy, and hope come to us—they are extended outward. Cranmer pulls us into a three-way conversation, between Christ, the sick, and those who accompany them. The prayer book enables us to know we are in this together. We are not alone, and through these three-way conversations, we are drawn closer into God's care.

Death came close again when a friend was diagnosed with stage four cancer. She was nearing fifty, her kids were teenagers, and whenever I went by their house her husband, Peter, looked at me with a stunned stare. His face seemed to ask, "What is happening? To us, to me, to our lives?"

The house felt like a hospital with its IV poles, paper masks, a commode in the bedroom. One of our clergy asked Anne if she'd like a few of us to come pray with her, and when she said yes, we met that Saturday. Two friends from Anne's work, whom I was fairly sure had spent little time in church, joined us. I wondered how this would be for them, and how it would be for Anne, watching them trying to pray alongside the rest of us.

As I got to her bed, Anne took my hand and gave it a squeeze. She had such lovely long fingers and beautiful rings. She shrugged and gave me a resigned smile. I wondered if she was not just getting ready to die but trying to help her friends get ready. Six of us pulled up chairs around her: me; one of our priests, Tom; Peter; another friend from church; and her two friends from work. The imminence of death often assembles odd collections of people.

The liturgy for the dying begins with God's words: Scripture verses. "The eternal God is your refuge, and underneath are the everlasting arms" (Deuteronomy 33:27). God will carry us. "Carry" is one of the most repeated verbs in the Scriptures and prayers for the sick and dying. We respond to God's commitment with the Lord's Prayer— it's our part in the conversation. It's meant to be a response. I noticed all of us said it, and I realized even with her head barely raised from the pillow, Anne was giving me the most subtle of grins. She saw that her friends were as relieved for the words as we were.

And then we said a responsive reading, a second tug into conversation with God, another plea for God to help and rescue Anne.

This service for the sick (as well as the services for the dying and the grieving) is back and forth, a dialogue of Scripture, prayer, Scripture, prayer. It's a subtle framework, not a monotonous one. You only see the continuing responsive pattern if you're looking.

Tom stopped for a minute, watching to see if Anne was okay. It was all feeling heavy. Then he moved us on to say the Apostles' Creed. At first it felt like a pledge of allegiance in a country that was not our own, but I realized as we said these ancient words that they were placed here as a comfort. In saying them, we can reroot ourselves in the solid foundation on which we live and die, the great Story of God's redemption, on the words "I believe in the resurrection of the body and the life everlasting."

Saying the Creed with Anne's friends reminded me of how the liturgy, particularly in moments of death and dying, can draw us into God's grace, even when its words are foreign or new to us. As people participate, they find themselves speaking far more "Christianly" than they think they are. By expressing our longing to affirm that God made the world and holds it together, that Christ goes before us, we relax.

These moments of finding ourselves drawn into these words always make me think of Dorothy Sayers' drama *The Zeal of Thy House*.[6] The play is a fictional account of the dialogue between God and the great twelfth-century architect William of Sens, when William was in charge of rebuilding Canterbury Cathedral after the fire that ruined much of the building. The underlying question is "Whose cathedral is it? God's or William's?" What's so remarkable about the way Sayers wrote the play is that as she unfolds the tension between the two, the audience finds themselves thinking as Christians. They, too, converse with God. The liturgy of the Book of Common Prayer can be much the same; Anne's friends were right with us, saying the prayers, saying the responses, saying the Creed. They seemed to cling to them. I think I caught Anne slyly raising an eyebrow in my direction. "Who knew?" her eyes seemed to marvel.

Tom asked us to lay our hands on Anne, and I wondered again if this was odd for her friends. But her coworkers placed their hands on her arm without hesitating, as if they wanted to, as if they might hold Anne back from death. I held her feet, trying not to tickle her toes. Her husband placed his hand on her hair—it was so gentle and so intimate, we all got teary. Tom placed his hand on her left arm and began:

> O ALMIGHTY God, whose blessed Son did lay his hands upon the sick and heal them: Grant, we beseech thee, to this thy servant on whom we now lay our hands in his Name, refreshment of spirit, and, according to thy gracious will, restoration to health of body and mind; through the same thy Son Jesus Christ our Lord. Amen.[7]

And then together we said,

> I LAY my hands on thee In the Name of our Saviour Jesus Christ, beseeching him that through his merits and precious death he will grant thee forgiveness of thy sins, relief from thy pains, and recovery of health in mind and body, to the glory of his Name. Amen.[8]

Tom continued,

> THE Almighty Lord, who is a most strong tower to all them that put their trust in him, to whom all things in heaven, in earth, and under the earth, do bow and obey: Be now and evermore thy defence; and make thee know and feel that there is none other name under heaven given to man, in whom, and through whom,

thou mayest receive health and salvation, but only the Name of our Lord Jesus Christ. Amen.[9]

The Laying On of Hands service is one of those acts that can sound as if it will be forced but feels easy, satiating, when we perform it. It's often our instinct. We want to join in showing our solidarity, and even better, we want to participate with the sick. We want to hold on to them, so they'll know they are not alone.

Anne smiled at us all, maybe trying to give us permission to let go, but I wasn't sure any of us wanted to. Pulling my hands off her feet felt like the first saying of goodbye.

Tom read us a collect for health:

ALMIGHTY God, giver of health and healing: Grant to this thy servant such a sense of thy presence that she may have perfect trust in thee. In all her suffering may she cast her care upon thee, so that, enfolded in thy love and power, she may receive from thee health and salvation according to thy gracious will; through Jesus Christ our Lord. Amen.[10]

We sat in silence, not wanting to be done, unsure what to say. I went back to Anne's to pray several more Saturdays; I'd have gone more if she'd wanted. It was better to pray than just worry.

Anne died about two months later.

The prayer book offers three services for those who have died. There is a full service for the burial (which I would call a "funeral" service). There is an additional liturgy for the graveside, and there's The Funeral for a Child. Several of the more recent versions of the prayer book have omitted the distinct service for a child, which seems like a loss. I love that Cranmer thought it was so important.

I have only attended a few funerals and burials that followed these services closely. Sadly, no one has ever included the option of Holy Communion. Picking and choosing from the prayers and readings seems to be more common. I understand this; we all want the service to be personal, particular to the person we love and miss, but I also sense that we are missing a means of grace that could soothe and hold our sadness. Isn't that the moment we most want to hear "This is my body, broken for you"?

The burial services for both adults and children are laden with Scripture readings. None is read more than John 11:25-26, "I am the resurrection and the life. The one who believes in me will live, even though they die; and whoever lives by believing in me will never die." I have come to see this as the moment in the conversation when God speaks, when he gives His definitive word.

Almost as frequent are Jesus' words shortly before his own death: "Do not let your hearts be troubled. You believe in God; believe also in me. My Father's house has many rooms; if that were not so, would I have told you that I am going there to prepare a place for you?" (John 14:1-2). Few realities are more comforting in death than knowing Christ Himself is preparing a home for us. The welcome mat will be out. The coffee will be hot.

Psalms 90, 121, and 130 are constants in the prayer book services (and in funerals in many denominations). These are consoling psalms, psalms of lament and sadness. I was recently at a service where portions of Psalm 90, as paraphrased in Eugene Peterson's *The Message,* were read.

> God, it seems you've been our home forever;
>> long before the mountains were born.
> Long before you brought earth itself to birth,
>> from "once upon a time" to "kingdom come"—you are God.
> So don't return us to mud, saying,
>> "Back to where you came from!"
> Patience! You've got all the time in the world—whether
>> a thousand years or a day, it's all the same to you.
> Surprise us with love at daybreak;
>> then we'll skip and dance all the day long.

Make up for the bad times with some good times;
    we've seen enough evil to last a lifetime.
Let your servants see what you're best at—
    the ways you rule and bless your children.
And let the loveliness of our Lord, our God, rest on us,
    confirming the work that we do.
    Oh, yes. Affirm the work that we do!
(Psalm 90:1-4, 14-17)[11]

The candor cheered me even in the sadness and finality of death. Our longing for God's affirmation is so deep; it felt good to have it voiced aloud.

Death drew close once again when my husband's parents died a day apart. At eighty-nine and ninety-two, they had been slipping away for the previous eighteen months. Craig's mother, Jan, had struggled with multiple sclerosis for fifty years and could no longer feed herself or speak. His dad, Hank, increasingly found it hard to walk, speak, and keep track of things. Their naps were longer and their appetites were smaller.

Early one afternoon the hospice worker called Craig to say that she thought his dad would die within weeks, possibly days. But the next afternoon, his mother, while sitting on the patio with her caregiver, lowered her head and breathed her last.

We raced to catch flights and arrived to be with his dad late that night. The next morning, while Hank slept late, we headed to the mortuary, planning to be back for an early lunch. Just as we were driving back to the house, we received a call that Hank had died too. His caregivers had woken him up around 10:00 a.m., and when he looked over at the empty side of the bed, he groaned, lay back, and twenty minutes later passed away. Physicians call this *takotsubo cardiomyopathy*, a heartbreaking emotional event that causes immense pressure on the left ventricle.

That afternoon the undertaker pulled up in his long black van to collect Craig's father's body. He was a burly fellow in his early thirties, well over six-foot-three, and I could see the tattoos under his sleeves and empty holes in his ears for his piercings. He quietly expressed his condolences, particularly having to be back at the house so soon. He was kind and didn't hesitate to slow down when Craig asked if we could pray over his dad before he took him away.

Craig got his prayer book, and we all stood around Hank, peaceful on the gurney, a sentimental blue blanket pulled up neatly to his shoulders, eyes open and face serene. The two caregivers looked stunned and uneasy. It was odd and momentous. Craig read to the five of us,

> O God, whose mercies cannot be numbered: Accept our prayers
> on behalf of thy servant, Henry, and grant him entrance into the
> land of light and joy, in the fellowship of thy saints; through
> Jesus Christ thy Son our Lord, who liveth and reigneth with thee
> and the Holy Spirit, one God, now and forever. Amen.[12]

Then Craig read Psalm 23, which his dad had loved, and finished with the Prayer of Commendation.

> Into your hands, O merciful Savior, we commend your servant,
> Henry. Acknowledge, we humbly beseech you, a sheep of your
> own fold, a lamb of your own flock, a sinner of your own re-
> deeming. Receive him into the arms of your mercy, into the
> blessed rest of everlasting peace, and into the glorious company
> of the saints in light. Amen.[13]

We all were quiet for a few seconds and then the undertaker looked to see if Craig was done. Craig nodded and as Hank's body was wheeled away, the two of us escaped to the patio.

A few minutes later the undertaker came to find us—he needed Craig to sign the myriad of forms. He looked down at Craig and asked, "Where did you get that thing you read?" Craig assumed he meant the psalm.

"It's in the Bible toward the middle. They are like poems."

The guy laughed nicely and said, "I know about the Psalms. No, I meant the prayer about the sheep. I've never heard it, and well, it's so true."

"Oh, the Prayer of Commendation. It's like a sendoff. It's in the Book of Common Prayer." Craig offered to take a photo of the short prayer, which our burly new friend seemed to truly want. He waited with us till it showed up on his phone.

"Thanks," he said. "I hear a lot of these kinds of things in my job—though it's funny how often people have no idea what to say—and well, even though the language sounds old, this rings true. You don't have to be religious to know that."

CONCLUSION
(*and* MORE SURPRISES)

*L*ike my beloved trees, with their seventeen different leaf shapes and countless varieties of flowers, there are innumerable facets of the prayer book I have yet to explore. I have yet to attend the Consecration of a Graveyard or a service of Midday Prayer. My chapters compose a short reflection on a very long book.

But in the time I have been writing these chapters, I have been humbled by the vast number of surprises that I have missed, not just in the Psalms but in all the prayer book's pages. I clearly have far more to learn.

When I first worshiped with the prayer book, I was in and out of graduate school, working and then raising children, then back in the workplace. In each of these seasons, the prayer book felt mysteriously relevant; it seemed to "get" me at just that moment. As I begin to venture from middle age to old, as four good friends have died in recent years, I am surprised by how much the prayer book has to teach me about death, about grief, and—maybe most importantly—about numbering my days.

I am surprised, too, by its ageless wisdom about our souls, how "spot on" (as a British friend describes it) it continues to be. While it sounds audacious, it strikes me that the prayer book is wiser than, say, Harvard's newest mental health research. The prayer book models taking our emotions seriously while never letting its words descend into a volcano of feelings. It models how we hold our hearts. The prayer book connects our emotion to occasion, to tangible experiences of longings for love and acceptance and hope, and where those longings are met.

But just as I am surprised at how the prayer book continues to feel personal, I am even more surprised by how relevant this 450-year-old book is to *us*, to our culture and moment in history. Cranmer compiled the prayer book to gather the church, to strengthen and unite Christians in prayer so they might be people who know and share the love and truth of Christ. I'm convinced North American Christians need this gathering and strengthening more than ever.

Within the Protestant church, one of our big temptations is mimicking the wider culture's passion for celebrity. We want famous people to attend our church, to validate our views. We cheer when our favorite filmmakers, musicians, and athletes are Christians. We want to be appealing. We gravitate toward famous pastors who attract more people. The prayer book goes a long way in keeping us from the worst of ourselves.

Another current temptation seems to be the church's yearning for newness, a new approach to worship or to meeting together, again with the goal of becoming more appealing. As Craig says, Christians are overly quick to feel we must "do more, try harder." We keep trying to assuage our fears of the church being seen as odd and irrelevant, and I would add that we keep forgetting the value and work of humble faithfulness, Scripture, and the prayer book's wisdom of living in the reality that our lives are, as Craig says, "all God's project." I see that these desires for relevance can bear terrific fruit, but at least as often they seem to distract us from focusing on loving and serving the people in our midst, from practicing forgiveness, from inviting others for lunch.

As theologian Stanley Hauerwas summed up, "The church is in a buyer's market that makes any attempt to form a disciplined congregational life very difficult."[1]

In this time of terrible divisiveness, Christians sadly seem to be nearly as divided among themselves. We rail against each other while the prayer book prods us to say the Lord's Prayer morning, noon, and night, asking God to help us to forgive our enemies, to keep us from the temptations of sin. As Tish Harrison Warren observes, the prayer book's words put us in a posture of prayer that can change us, inspire us. "My heart," she says, "through prayer, begins imagining a kind of ethic of forgiveness that my conscious will can't yet reach."[2] While the prayer book is not a panacea for divisiveness (nor are Anglicans or Episcopalians any better about this problem), daily use of the prayer book, saying the Lord's Prayer two or three times each day, offers a humble and united foundation.

But the prayer book's biggest surprise in its enduring relevance is how it speaks to the reality of what church *is*, of what it is meant to be in each of our lives. I keep meeting Christians who have given up going to church; they seem to see it as optional. Some don't seem to know what Scripture has to say about it. They have forgotten, or never knew, that Christ gave us the church as His treasured gift, to bless and to hold us, to belong to, to care for us until He returns. He wants us there, together. Participating in church is part of following Jesus.

Just as it did nearly five hundred years ago, the prayer book walks through what church *is*—what it is to be the body of Christ. It walks us through worship, through all that God has revealed to us in His Word. It offers a script for doing things together in a way that builds our communities, celebrates our meals and milestones, connects us to each other, and roots us in the wonderful love of Christ. It holds us together not just with those praying in Rio, Rotterdam, and Reno, but also with those in Nairobi, New York, and Naples.

The prayer book not only surprises us, it situates us in God's story over and over again. It helps us notice, learn, and remember, together.

ACKNOWLEDGMENTS

*F*irst, and perhaps most important, my enormous thanks to the people (my people!) of St. John's—the congregation past and present, the staff and clergy. This book and these experiences would not have happened without watching you sink to your knees, hearing you say the words of the Confession Sunday after Sunday, standing beside you as you're given the bread and wine, witnessing the ways you live out the gospel. Being with you in the hard stuff and the high points has been among the great pleasures and privileges of my life. Thank you.

I am embarrassed at the sheer number of people needed to make this book happen but astounded by and grateful for God's care for me in the quality of their skills and support.

Lauren Winner, your early enthusiasm and fantastic editorial input was a game-changer. Thank you.

Kasey Kimball, your friendship, edits, theological wisdom, and ongoing cheerleading have blessed me beyond measure.

Karen Stiller and Arthur Boers, your support, advice, input, and confidence have been such generous gifts. Thank you.

Ethan McCarthy, your willingness to take a chance on me, followed by your skilled editing, theological wisdom, and well-placed encouragement, have been gifts in themselves. Thank you. I hope I have made you proud.

Rachel Howard, I would not and could not have written this without your encouragement and exceptional skills. Thank you *so* much.

Bethany Murphy, your eleventh-hour editing and encouragement were fantastic. I appreciate both enormously.

Don Pape, being a sheep of your flock is the best. A privilege and a pleasure. Thank you for everything.

So many friends have been supportive—thank you all. Some of you have read chapters at needed moments, others have offered ongoing support, and others have said a few words that made such a difference: Kim, Lesley, Karen, Thena, Maxine, Elise, Trish and Carrie, Ron, Jana, Lindi, Pat, George, Keith, Jen, Lucila, Vivian, Zella, Sarah, Kathy, Trish, and Carolyn. Thank you all.

Uncle Dr. P., for all the ways you encouraged me—thank you. I await your feedback. Don Lewis, Bruce Hindmarsh, thank you for keeping me accurate and sharing the depths of the prayer book. Loren Wilkinson, Bruce Waltke, Jim Houston, Iain Provan, Gordon Smith, Gordon Fee, Eugene Peterson—thank you for all the ways you have strengthened my trust in His goodness all the days of my life.

Raquel Boleza, thank you for enabling my work, for providing endless hospitality, for your stupendous care.

Mom and Dad, there will never be enough times or places to express my gratitude, for being such wonderful people and so loving and loyal to me—thank you, thank you.

Whitney, world's kindest sister, thank you for receiving the collects with such enthusiasm and for sending them right back, for cheering me on so well, particularly in the final months.

Andrew, Casey, Elsa, Owen, Nick, Sam, and Peter—for hearing you say the Confession, Grace, or the Lord's Prayer beside me, for all the times one of you prompted me to pull out my prayer book—in worry, care, repentance, and thanks—thank you. I love each of you so much.

Rod and Ruth, for your steadfast friendship, encouragement in Christ, the endless ways you have supported and participated—you are two of God's most wonderful gifts.

Susie and Connally, your time, guidance, brilliance, wisdom, and editing have been a gigantic gift of friendship to me. You made this book so much better than it might have been. Susie, you embraced my project as a fascinating adventure, and it's made the work infinitely more fun. Thank you.

Finlay, thank you for racing to the loft to check on me, for all the ways you embodied God's love for me.

Craig, for taking church so seriously, for patience with this project (and so much else), for sharing your wonderful brilliance, for the immense love and life you have given me so faithfully and for so long—thank you.

NOTES

INTRODUCTION

[1] Lesslie Newbigin, *Proper Confidence: Faith, Doubt and Certainty in Christian Discipleship* (Grand Rapids, MI: Eerdmans, 1995), 76.

[2] The 1962 Canadian Book of Common Prayer can be found in its entirety at https:// prayerbook.ca.

1. MORNING AND EVENING PRAYER

[1] Tim Challies, "What Not to Say at the Beginning of a Worship Service," *Challies* (blog), September 16, 2019, www.challies.com/articles/what-not-to-say-at-the -beginning-of-a-worship-service/.

[2] Tish Harrison Warren, "Putting the Poetry Back in Christmas," interview with Malcolm Guite, *New York Times*, December 11, 2022, www.nytimes.com/2022/12/11 /opinion/advent-christmas-poetry.html?searchResultPosition=15.

[3] Anglican Church in North America, *The Book of Common Prayer with the New Coverdale Psalter* (Huntington Beach, CA: Anglican Liturgy Press, 2019), 41-42, abbreviated as ACNA 2019 in following notes.

[4] Laura Smith, "Charles to Repent 'Manifold Sins,'" *The Guardian*, April 8, 2005, www .theguardian.com/uk/2005/apr/08/monarchy.laurasmith.

[5] Eugene Peterson, introduction to the first edition, *Epiphanies: Stories for the Christian Year*, ed. Eugene Peterson and Emilie Griffin (Grand Rapids, MI: Baker Books, 2003), 7.

[6] James K. A. Smith, *You Are What You Love: The Spiritual Power of Habit* (Grand Rapids, MI: Brazos, 2016), 47.

[7] ACNA 2019, 12.

[8] Noah Van Neil, "What Is to Become of Confession?," *Covenant Living Church* (blog), January 8, 2018, https://covenant.livingchurch.org/2018/01/08/what-is -to-become-of-the-confession/.

[9] ACNA 2019, 13.

[10] Tish Harrison Warren, *Liturgy of the Ordinary: Sacred Practices in Everyday Life* (Downers Grove, IL: InterVarsity Press, 2016), 59.

[11] ACNA 2019, 13.

[12] *The Book of Common Prayer: and Administration of the Sacraments and Other Rites and Ceremonies of the Church According to the Use of the Anglican Church of Canada* (Toronto: Anglican Book Centre, 1962), 11-12, abbreviated as CAN 1962 in following notes.

[13] CAN 1962, 14-15.

[14] Alan Jacobs, *The Book of Common Prayer: A Biography* (Princeton, NJ: Princeton University Press, 2013), 106.

[15] Schlitz Beer, "You Only Go Around Once in Life," 1970, https://propadv.com/alcohol-ad-and-poster-collection/schlitz-ad-and-poster-collection/1970-you-only-go-around-once-in-life-so-grab-for-all-the-gusto-you-can-schlitz-3/.

[16] Busch Brewing, "Head for the Mountains," 1978, www.youtube.com/watch?v=aEqjeKmdsqk.

[17] Miller Brewing Company, "If You've Got the Time, We've Got the Beer," 1979, www.youtube.com/watch?v=vgys7Rjdw3Y.

[18] Jessie Adams, "I Feel the Winds of God Today," 1893. Tune unverifiable.

[19] ACNA 2019, 63, 48.

2. THE COLLECTS

[1] CAN 1962, 11-12.

[2] Henry Ossawa Tanner, *The Good Shepherd*, 1922, oil on canvas, 32 in. x 23.625 in., Newark Museum of Art.

[3] CAN 1962, 136.

[4] J. I. Packer, "Rooted and Built Up in Christ (Col. 2:6-7): The Prayer Book Path," (lecture, Prayer Book Society of Canada, St. Paul's Church, Toronto, ON, May 1, 1999), https://prayerbook.ca/j-i-packer-the-prayer-book-path/.

[5] CAN 1962, 321.

[6] CAN 1962, 323.

[7] ACNA 2019, 671.

[8] ACNA 2019, 63.

[9] CAN 1962, 730-31.

[10] CAN 1962, 67.

[11] Frederick Buechner, *Clown in the Belfry: Writings on Faith and Fiction* (San Francisco: HarperSanFrancisco, 1992), 122.

[12] ACNA 2019, 598.

3. PRAYERS FOR FAMILIES AND INDIVIDUALS

[1] I secretly feared we were the only couple who failed to pray together regularly but I have slowly learned (largely through sharing our use of Family Prayers as a "solution,") it's quite common. I was especially comforted when I read Tim Keller's admission that "about nine years ago Kathy and I were contemplating the fact that we had largely failed to pray together over the years." (Timothy Keller, "Scraps of Thoughts on Daily Prayer," *Timothy Keller* [blog], July 13, 2010, https://timothykeller.com/blog/2010/7/13/scraps-of-thoughts-on-daily-prayer.)

[2] CAN 1962, 729-29.

[3] ACNA 2019, 67-78; CAN 1962, 728-36.

[4] Edmund Gibson, *Family-Devotion: Or, An Exhortation to Morning and Evening Prayer in Families*, 18th ed. (London: reprinted from T. Hatchard, 1858), 1.

[5] Gibson, *Family-Devotion*, 1.

[6] Gibson, *Family-Devotion*, 3-4.

[7] CAN 1962, 128.

[8] CAN 1962, 729.

[9] CAN 1962, 729.

[10] CAN 1962, 729 (2 Corinthians 13:14).

[11] Tish Harrison Warren, *Prayers in the Night: For Those Who Work or Watch or Weep* (Downers Grove, IL: InterVarsity Press, 2021), 9.

[12] CAN 1962, 730.

[13] CAN 1962, 730.

[14] CAN 1962, 730.

[15] CAN 1962, 730-31.

[16] CAN 1962, 731.

[17] CAN 1962, 731.

4. LITURGICAL YEAR

[1] Joan Chittister, *The Liturgical Year: The Spiraling Adventure of the Spiritual Life* (Nashville: Thomas Nelson, 2009), 27.

[2] Malcolm Guite, "History of the Church Year," (lecture, Regent College, Vancouver, BC, July 17, 2015).

[3] David Roseberry, "For the Beauty of the Year: The Liturgical Calendar," Anglican Compass, November 22, 2016, https://anglicancompass.com/liturgical-calendar/.

[4] ACNA 2019, 676.

[5] Phillips Brooks, "O Little Town of Bethlehem," (Christmas carol), 1868, public domain.

[6] ACNA 2019, 604.

[7] Ron Rolheiser, "Entering Lent," *Ron Rolheiser* (blog), February 22, 2009, https://ronrolheiser.com/entering-lent/#.ZDmgH-zMIq8.

[8] ACNA 2019, 606.

[9] C. S. Lewis, *The Weight of Glory* (New York: Macmillan, 1949), 1.

[10] Virginia Stem Owens, "Good Friday" in *Epiphanies: Stories for the Christian Year*, ed. Eugene Peterson and Emilie Griffin (Grand Rapids, MI: Baker Books, 2003), 130.

[11] N. T. Wright, *Surprised by Hope: Rethinking Heaven, the Resurrection and the Mission of the Church* (New York: HarperOne, 2008), 256.

[12] Chittister, *Liturgical Year*, 99.

[13] Gordon J. Brown, "A Lectionary of Eating: Reflections on the Centrality of Eating to the Rhythms of Creation's Seasonal Cycle and the Church's Liturgical Year," *CRUX* 48, no. 2 (Winter 2012): 13.

[14] Eugene Peterson, *A Long Obedience in the Same Direction: Discipleship in an Instant Society* (Downers Grove, IL: InterVarsity Press, 1980).

[15] Wendell Berry, "Manifesto: The Farmers Mad Liberation Front," in *The Selected Poems of Wendell Berry* (San Francisco: Counterpoint Press, 1999).

5. PSALMS

[1] Kathleen Norris, *The Cloister Walk* (New York: Riverhead Books, 1996), 100.

[2] Derek Kidner, *Psalms 1-72*, Kidner Classic Commentaries (Downers Grove, IL: IVP Academic, 2014), 42.

[3] Eno Adeogun, "Bono Speaks on the Psalms," Premier Christian News, May 18, 2017, https://premierchristian.news/en/news/article/bono-speaks-of-lessons-learnt-through-psalms.

[4] David Taylor, "How to Read the Psalms for All They're Worth," Anglican Compass, February 27, 2020, https://anglicancompass.com/how-to-read-the-psalms-for-all-theyre-worth/.

[5] Samuel L. Bray, "Reading Psalm 137 in Church," Confessing Anglicans, https://confessinganglicans.com/reading-psalm-137-in-church/.

[6] C. S. Lewis, *Reflections on the Psalms* (New York and London: Harcourt, Brace and Jovanovich, 1958), 93-97.

[7] Eugene Peterson, *Leap Over A Wall* (New York: Harper Collins, 1997), 152.

[8] Iain Provan, "The Psalms and Torah," (lecture, Regent College, Vancouver, BC, January 13, 2021).

6. BAPTISM

[1] "Tofino Whale-Watching Accident Leads Residents to Gather for Support," CBC News, October 26, 2015, www.cbc.ca/1.3288391.

[2] Alan Jacobs, *The Book of Common Prayer: A Biography* (Princeton, NJ: Princeton University Press, 2013), 92.

[3] "O Love That Will Not Let Me Go" is sung in two (or more) different tunes. I highly recommend the Indelible Grace version.

[4] Henry Ives Bailey, *The Liturgy as Compared to the Bible*, vol. 1, 1830, public domain.

[5] N. T. Wright, "N. T. Wright on Word and Sacraments: Baptism (Part 2 of 3)," *Reformed Worship* 90 (January 2008), www.reformedworship.org/article/december-2008 /n-t-wright-word-and-sacraments-baptism.

[6] Tish Harrison Warren, *Liturgy of the Ordinary: Sacred Practices in Everyday Life* (Downers Grove, IL: InterVarsity Press, 2016), 17.

7. COMPLINE

[1] ACNA 2019, 57.

[2] Ellis Peters, *The Leper of Saint Giles* (London, UK: MacMillan London Ltd., 1981), 98.

[3] Church of England, *An Order for Night Prayer (Compline)*, www.churchofengland .org/prayer-and-worship/worship-texts-and-resources/common-worship/daily -prayer/night-prayer-compline.

[4] Church of England, *Order for Night Prayer*.

[5] Malcolm Guite, quoted in "Malcolm Guite to Deliver 2019 Laing Lectures, April 9-11," January 31, 2019, www.regent-college.edu/about-us/news/2019/malcolm-guite -to-deliver-2019-laing-lectures--april-911. This could also be attributed to William Shakespeare, *A Midsummer Night's Dream*, Act 5, Scene 1.

[6] Church of England, *Order for Night Prayer*.

8. THE CATECHISM

[1] Jen Wilkin, foreword to *God of All Things*, by Andrew Wilson (Grand Rapids, MI: Zondervan, 2021), xii.

[2] Anglican Church in North America, *To Be a Christian: An Anglican Catechism* (Newport Beach, CA: Anglican House Publishers, 2013), Q:56, 44.

[3] James K. A. Smith, *You Are What You Love: The Spiritual Power of Habit* (Grand Rapids, MI: Brazos Press, 2016), 19.

[4] Jill Suttie, "How Smartphones Are Killing Conversation: A Q&A with MIT Professor Sherry Turkle," *Greater Good Magazine*, December 7, 2015, https://greatergood .berkeley.edu/article/item/how_smartphones_are_killing_conversation. See also Veronica V. Galván, Rosa S. Vessal, and Matthew T. Golley, "The Effects of Cell Phone Conversations on the Attention and Memory of Bystanders," National Library of Medicine, March 13, 2013, www.ncbi.nlm.nih.gov/pmc/articles /PMC3596270/.

[5] Josh Retterer, "What I Stand On: Wendell Berry's Collected Catechisms," *Mockingbird*, July 17, 2019, https://mbird.com/literature/what-i-stand-on-wendell-berrys -collected-catechisms/.

[6] Wendell Berry, "Questionnaire," *Leavings* (New York: Macmillan, 2010), 14. Used by permission.

[7] *The New City Catechism*, http://newcitycatechism.com/.

[8] George Herbert, *The Country Parson, The Temple*, ed. with an introduction by John N. Wall Jr. (New York: Paulist Press, 1981), 84.

[9] ACNA 1962, 545.

[10] ACNA, *To Be a Christian*, Q:56, 44.

[11] Jeremy Begbie, "How Music Helps Explain the Trinity," June 15, 2016, *Seven Minute Seminary* (podcast), https://seedbed.com/how-music-helps-explain-the-trinity/.

[12] ACNA, *To Be a Christian*, Q:100, 58.

[13] "Things," (Laing Lecture, Regent College, Vancouver, BC, March 8, 2023).

[14] Brett Foster, "Catechism," *Christianity and Literature* 58, no. 2 (Winter 2009): 211. Used by permission.

[15] ACNA, *To Be a Christian*, Q:263, 113.

[16] ACNA, *To Be a Christian*, Q:322, 123.

[17] Charles Colcock Jones quoted in Alex Fogleman, "Manipulating Catechesis: A Note of Caution," Anglican Compass, November 19, 2020, https://anglicancompass.com /manipulating-catechesis-a-note-of-caution/.

[18] CAN 1962, 549-50.

[19] CAN 1962, 555.

9. HOLY COMMUNION

[1] Henri J. M. Nouwen, *With Burning Hearts: A Meditation on Eucharistic Life* (Maryknoll, NY: Orbis Books, 1994), 67.

[2] CAN 1962, 67.

[3] Flannery O'Connor, "Revelation," in *The Complete Stories of Flannery O'Connor* (New York: Farrar, Straus and Giroux, 1946), 506.

[4] Lauren F. Winner, *A Word to Live By: Church's Teaching for a Changing World* (New York: Church Publishing, 2017), 49.

[5] CAN 1962, 76.

[6] CAN 1962, 77.

[7] Samuel L. Bray and Drew Nathaniel Keane, eds., *The 1662 Book of Common Prayer: International Edition* (Downers Grove, IL: IVP Academic, 2022), 749.

[8] Nouwen, *With Burning Hearts*, 67.

[9] ACNA 2019, 119.

[10] Terry Waite, "A Very Present Help in Trouble," in *The Book of Common Prayer: Past, Present, & Future*, ed. Prudence Dailey (London: Continuum, 2011), 195.

[11] Nora Gallagher, *The Sacred Meal* (Nashville: Thomas Nelson, 2009), 56.

[12] ACNA 2019, 137.

10. IN SICKNESS AND IN DEATH

[1] CAN 1962, 574.

[2] CAN 1962, 574-75.

[3] ACNA 2019, 232.

[4] CAN 1962, 605.

[5] CAN 1962, 606.

[6] Dorothy L. Sayers, *The Zeal of Thy House* (London: Victor Gollancz, 1937).

[7] CAN 1962, 584.

[8] CAN 1963, 584-5.

[9] CAN 1962, 585.

[10] CAN 1962, 580.

[11] Eugene Peterson, *The Message* (Colorado Springs, CO: Navigators Publishing Group, 2015), 1026-27.

[12] The Episcopal Church, *The Book of Common Prayer and Administrations of the Sacraments and Other Rites and Ceremonies of the Church* (New York: Oxford University Press, 2007), 470.

[13] The Episcopal Church, *The Book of Common Prayer*, 483.

CONCLUSION (AND MORE SURPRISES)

[1] Stanley Hauerwas, *Approaching the End: Eschatological Reflections on Church, Politics, and Life* (Grand Rapids, MI: Eerdmans, 2013), 82.

[2] Tish Harrison Warren, "By the Book," *Comment*, December 1, 2016, https://comment.org/by-the-book/.

SUGGESTED GUIDES
to the BOOK *of*
COMMON PRAYER

*I*f you want a guide, or to learn more about the prayer book or the Anglican church, the following have been helpful to me.

Bevins, Winfield H. *Our Common Prayer: A Field Guide to the Book of Common Prayer*. USA: Simeon Press, 2013; and *Simply Anglican: An Ancient Faith for Today's World*. Prosper, TX: Anglican Compass, 2020. Welcoming, relevant introductions for those trying to find their bearings.

Bray, Samuel L., and Drew Nathaniel Keane. *How to Use the Book of Common Prayer: A Guide to the Anglican Liturgy*. Downers Grove, IL: InterVarsity Press, 2024. An excellent overview and guide, written for newcomers but interesting to those more knowledgeable as well.

Careless, Sue. *Discovering the Book of Common Prayer: A Hands-On Approach*. 3 vols. Toronto, ON: ABC Publishing, 2006. Volume 1 gives an overview of the liturgy and a deep dive into the four services of the day; volume 2 focuses on Baptism, Holy Communion, Confirmation, and Catechism; volume 3 looks at the services for Marriage, Sickness, Death, Ordination, and some of the lesser-known services. While these were written for Canadians (using the 1962 and 1985 prayer books), these three are the most user-friendly, helpful, and well-researched of all guides. Sue Careless answers what many will feel are the "dumb question, but . . ." inquiries better than anyone.

Jacobs, Alan. *The Book of Common Prayer: A Biography*. Princeton, NJ: Princeton University Press, 2013. Covers the prayer book's history from its Anglican beginnings in the 1500s to its use across the world in 2010.

McPherson, C.W. *Grace at This Time: Praying the Daily Office.* Harrisburg, PA: Morehouse Publishing, 1999. A lesser-known gem by an Episcopal priest, guiding the reader through the Episcopal services of Morning Prayer, Noonday Prayer, Evening Prayer, and Compline with kindness, knowledge, and humor.

Olson, Derek. *Inwardly Digest: The Prayer Book as Guide to Spiritual Life.* Cincinnati, OH: Forward Movement Cincinnati, 2016. A practical guide, an overview, and, as the title says, a way to connect our spiritual lives to the liturgy when we are new to the prayer book. It's readable and very accessible.

Packer, J. I. *The Gospel in the Prayer Book.* Appleford, UK: Markham Manor Press, 1966. Reprint, Downers Grove, IL: IVP Academic, 2021. In combination with Henry Ives Bailey's astounding 1830s three volumes, *The Liturgy Compared with the Bible,* in which Bailey ties almost every word of Cranmer's liturgy to specific Scripture verses, these are the books to find where the prayer book originates.

Thomas, Paul. *Using the Book of Common Prayer: A Simple Guide.* London, UK: Church House Publishing, 2012. Exactly as its title suggests: a short, straightforward guide.

Fullness of Time series. Downers Grove, IL: InterVarsity Press, 2023. These titles invite readers to journey through the church year as church theologians explore the traditions, prayers, Scriptures, and rituals of a season of the church.

 **IVP formatio**

BECOMING OUR TRUE SELVES

The nautilus is one of the sea's oldest creatures. Beginning with a tight center, its remarkable growth pattern can be seen in the ever-enlarging chambers that spiral outward. The nautilus in the IVP Formatio logo symbolizes deep inward work of spiritual formation that begins rooted in our souls and then opens to the world as we experience spiritual transformation. The shell takes on a stunning pearlized appearance as it ages and forms in much the same way as the souls of those who devote themselves to spiritual practice. Formatio books draw on the ancient wisdom of the saints and the early church as well as the rich resources of Scripture, applying tradition to the needs of contemporary life and practice.

Within each of us is a longing to be in God's presence. Formatio books call us into our deepest desires and help us to become our true selves in the light of God's grace.

LIKE THIS BOOK?

Scan the code to discover more content like this!

Get on IVP's email list to receive special offers, exclusive book news, and thoughtful content from your favorite authors on topics you care about.

IVPRESS.COM/BOOK-QR